WHERE THE GHOSTS ARE:

Favorite Haunted Houses in America and the British Isles

Books by Hans Holzer

Non-Fiction

The Aquarian Age
Astrology: What It Can Do for
    You
Beyond Medicine
Beyond this Life
Charismatics
The Directory of the Occult
Elvis Presley Speaks (From the
    Beyond)
ESP and You
Ghost Hunter
Ghosts I've Met
The Ghosts that Walk in
    Washington
Gothic Ghosts
The Habsburg Curse
The Handbook of
    Parapsychology
Hans Holzer's Haunted Houses
Haunted Hollywood
Hidden Meanings in Dreams
Houses of Horror
How to Win at Life
The Human Dynamo
Inside Witchcraft
Life After Death: the Challenge
    and the Evidence
Murder in Amityville
Patterns of Destiny
Phantoms of Dixie
The Power of Hypnosis
The Powers of the New Age

The Primer of Reincarnation
The Prophets Speak
Psychic Healing
The Psychic Side of Dreams
Psycho-Ecstasy
Some of My Best Friends Are
    Ghosts
Speed Thinking
Star Ghosts
The Truth About ESP
The Truth About Witchcraft
The UFOnauts: New Facts on
    Extraterrestrial Landings
The Vegetarian Way of Life
Window to the Past
The Witchcraft Report
Yankee Ghosts

Fiction

The Alchemist
The Alchemy Deception
The Amityville Curse
Circle of Love
The Clairvoyant
The Entry
Heather, Confessions of a Witch
The Red Chindvit Conspiracy
Star of Destiny
The Unicorn
The Zodiac Affairs

WHERE THE GHOSTS ARE:

Favorite Haunted Houses in America and the British Isles

Hans Holzer

Parker Publishing Company, Inc.
West Nyack, New York

Library of Congress Cataloging in Publication Data

Holzer, Hans.
　Where the ghosts are.

　1. Ghosts—United States. 2. Ghosts—Great Britain.
I. Title.
BF1472.U6H639 1984　　　133.1′2973　　　84-14779

ISBN 0-13-957093-4

ISBN 0-13-957077-2 {PBK}

Printed in the United States of America

FOREWORD

I was lying on the sun roof of the Hyatt-on-Sunset Hotel in West Hollywood, drying myself after a nice, vigorous swim, when two strange-looking young men emerged from below and approached me in a purposeful fashion: they wanted to talk to me!

Now, I wouldn't mind being sought out by two lovely young ladies, (there are always some around the swimming pool at the Hyatt and I don't even mind someone wanting my autograph or wanting to tell me about a favorite haunted house they'd heard about. But there was something very odd about those two fellows who had now reached my comfortable chair. Their faces were as white as sheets, and for a fleeting moment I encouraged the thought that they were indeed a couple of ghosts risen from very far below to challenge me (or perhaps only to be included in one of my next books).

But they were not ghosts after all. They were rock musicians who had just gotten up in the middle of the day. They had heard I was staying at the Hyatt-on-Sunset, and they did want to tell me about a house in the Hollywood hills where they had encountered some eerie goings on—not the kind musicians are used to, but something more along my lines of expertise.

As I continued to take the sun in my chair, I became convinced that the time had come to do a book for all those eager people who are fascinated by haunted houses and ghosts and are simply not satisfied with hearing about them . . . but choose to seek them out as well.

The two young men left me soon afterwards, and the haunted house in the hills turned out to be one I had already visited years ago.

When I went back to New York, where I normally live—well, as normally as one in my position can—I thought of writing a guide and travel book dealing with the kind of places you don't see listed in Fodor's or Baedecker's simply because their authors wouldn't know where to find them even if they believed they existed . . . which they probably don't. Places with resident spooks in them, places where there are what I like to call stay-behinds—people who stay in what used to be their homes long after their physical bodies have disintegrated through death—places with "something extra" in them are usually private and inaccessible to the curious. But there are some that are public places, such as museums, manor houses, palaces, churches, and, of course, hotels and inns. Enough of those public or quasi-public places, and a handful of private ones whose owners might just allow an occasional visitor, would be the heart of one of my next books.

When I returned to West hollywood and the Hyatt Hotel again, I started to make a list of such places, including of course many in California wihtin hours of my hotel room—the Whaley House in San Diego, the house where Carole Lombard's ghost appeared, the former residence of the Barrymores on Summit Drive, and many more. During my stay at the Hyatt, many leading psychics came to see me, to read for me, and some to drop hints at maybe still another house in the hills I ought to have a look at. Fabulously successful soothsayers as Sherri Sidebottom, Anni Pignatelli and Monique Collins, fellow researchers as Dr. Eugene Jussek, and my dearest friend and fellow Aquarian, London writer-comedian Michael Bentine, all spent time with me in my 7th floor room in what used to be the Continental Hyatt House, when I first came there 15 years ago.

I hope you like the results of my efforts.

Hans Holzer

CONTENTS

FOREWORD 5

I. WHAT IS A GHOST? 9

II. ARE THERE SUCH THINGS AS "LIVING" GHOSTS? .. 23

III. HOW TO LIVE WITH A POLTERGEIST 29

IV. PUBLIC HOUSES, AMERICA 39

1. The Whaley House, California 41
2. The Ghostly Stagecoach Inn, Thousand Oaks,
   California 44
3. The Haunted Organ at Yale University,
   New Haven, Connecticut 46
4. John Wilkes Booth's Tavern, Clinton, Maryland 49
5. The Ghost at the Ship Chandlery, Massachusetts ... 52
6. The Ocean-Born Mary House, New Hampshire 54
7. The "Spy House" Ghosts, New Jersey 58
8. The Ghost Servants of Ringwood Manor,
   New Jersey 63
9. The Conference House Ghosts, New York City 66
10. Aaron Burr's Haunted Stables, New York City 75
11. The Old Merchant's House Ghosts,
    New York City 78
12. The Ghosts at the Jumel-Morris Mansion,
    New York City 81
13. The Ghosts at St. Mark's in the Bouwerie,
    New York City 86
14. A Ghost in Greenwich Village, New York City 88
15. The Haunting at the Poughkeepsie Rectory,
    New York State 93
16. The Ghost at West Point, New York State 95
17. The Ghost at the Altar, Pennsylvania 98
18. Lincoln's Ghost, Washington, D.C. 101
19. The Ghosts at the Octagon, Washington, D.C. 108
20. Haunted Fort McNair, Washington, D.C. 112
21. The Ghostly Rocking Chair, Ash Lawn, Virginia ...115
22. Haunted Michie Tavern, Virginia 117
23. The Haunting in the Postmaster's House,
    Virginia 121

24. Jefferson's Spirit at Monticello, Virginia 124
25. Westover's Evelyn, Virginia 127
26. The Howard Mansion, Texas 131
27. The Haunted Nightclub of Toronto 134
28. Rose Hall, Home of the "White Witch"
    of Jamaica 136

V. HAUNTED LOCATIONS, AMERICA 139

29. The Haunted Lady of Nob Hill, San Francisco,
    California 141
30. Haunted Clinton Court, New York City 144
31. The Haunted Frigate *Constellation*, Baltimore,
    Maryland 147
32. The Ghostly Maco Light, North Carolina 150

VI. PRIVATE GHOST HOUSES, AMERICA 153

33. The Haunted Hollywood Party, California 155
34. The Stamford Hills Ghosts, Connecticut 159
35. The Haunted Basement, Georgia 163
36. The Indian Girl Ghost of Kentucky 168
37. The Haunted Trailer, Massachusetts 171
38. The Phantom Admiral, New Hampshire 174
39. The Little Old Lady Ghost of Bank Street,
    New York City 177
40. June Havoc's Haunted Town House,
    New York City 180
41. The Case of the Tipsy Ghost, New York City 182
42. Lucy, and Her Virginia House Ghosts 185

VII. HOUSES IN THE BRITISH ISLES 189

43. The Nell Gwyn House, London 191
44. Hall Place, Kent 193
45. The Tower, London 195
46. The Garrick's Head Inn, Bath 197
47. The Ghostly Monks at Beaulieu, Hampshire 199
48. Longleat Palace, Bath 202
49. Salisbury Hall, St. Albans 205
50. Sawston Hall, Cambridge 208
51. Hermitage Castle, Scotland 211
52. Carlingford Abbey, Ireland 215
53. Renvyle, Connemara 217
54. Kilkea Castle, Kildare 219

WHERE THE GHOSTS ARE:

Favorite Haunted Houses in America and the British Isles

I
What Is a Ghost?

What exactly is a ghost? Before I wrote *Ghost Hunter*, my first book, in 1962, the question might have been an academic one or a controversial one, depending on one's point of view. When the question of haunted houses came up in polite conversation, people were generally split into two uneven groups: the majority, who thought the notion that there were indeed such things as ghosts was amusing, if not preposterous; and a tiny but interested minority who believed that that was indeed possible.

Ever since the dawn of mankind, people have believed in ghosts. The fear of the unknown, the certainty that there was something somewhere out there, bigger than life, beyond its pale, and more powerful than anything walking the earth, has persisted throughout the ages. It had its origins in primitive man's thinking. To him, there were good and evil forces at work in nature, both ruled over by supernatural beings, and to some degree capable of being influenced by the attitudes and prayers of man. The fear of death was, of course, one of the strongest human emotions. It is still. Although some belief in survival after physical death has existed from the beginning of time, no one ever cherished the notion of leaving this earth. Thus death represented a menace.

An even greater threat was the return of those known to be dead. In the French language, ghosts are referred to as *les revenants*—that is to say, the returning ones. To the majority of people, ghosts are those coming back from the realms of the dead to haunt the living for one or another reason. I am still being asked by interviewers why such-and-such a person came back as a ghost. My psychic research and my many books published since 1962 have of course refuted the notion that ghosts are *returnees* from the land of the dead. Every indication drawn from direct interrogation of those who have had experiences of a psychic nature, as well as communications with the so-called "other side of life," has indicated to me that ghosts are not travelers in any sense of the word.

Then what are ghosts—if, indeed, there *are* such things? To the materialist and the professional skeptic—that is, people who do not wish to be disturbed in their belief that death is the end of life as we know it—the notion of ghosts is unacceptable. No matter how much evidence is presented for the reality of the phenomenon, they will argue against it and ascribe it to any of several "natural" causes. Either delusion or hallucination must be the explanation, or perhaps a mirage, if not outright trickery on the part of parties unknown. Entire professional groups who deal in the manufacture of illusions have taken it upon themselves to label anything that defies their ability to reproduce it artificially through trickery or manipulation as false or nonexistent. Especially among photographers and magicians, the notion that ghosts exist has never been a popular one. But authentic reports of psychic phenomena along ghostly lines keep coming into reputable report centers such as the various societies for psychic research, or to people who are parapsychologists like myself.

Granted that a certain number of these reports may be due to inaccurate reporting, self-delusion, or other errors of fact, there still remains an impressive number of cases that cannot be explained by any other means than that of extrasensory perception.

In this book I do not tell my readers of legends or unconfirmed sightings, or of romanticized stories of ghosts that walk only at certain times but at no other. Many such reports have a basis in fact, but unfortunately, in these cases, that basis has never been verified by me or anyone whose word I can accept as reputable.

Frequently, various tourist organizations pounce upon media reports of ghostly occurrences to build them into tourist-attracting stories. While this is certainly not harmful to anyone—least of all the ghosts if there are real ones on the premises—it does not lend itself to the kind of verifiable, scientific effort I am interested in, nor does it promise a casual visitor to the place the remote possibility of a personal encounter with a phantom even if he is possessed of extrasensory perception.

What exactly is a ghost? In terms of psychic research, as I have defined them, a ghost appears to be a surviving emotional memory of someone who has died traumatically, and usually tragically, but is unaware of his death. Ghosts, then, in the overwhelming majority, do not realize that they are dead. Those who do know they are "dead" are confused as to where they are, or why they feel not quite as they used to feel. When death occurs unexpectedly or unacceptably, or when a person has lived in a place for a very long time, acquiring certain routine habits and becoming very attached to the premises, sudden, unexpected death may come as a shock. Unwilling to part with the physical world, such human personalities then continue to stay on in the very spot where their tragedy or their emotional attachment had existed prior to physical death.

Ghosts do not travel; they do not follow people home; nor do they appear at more than one place. Nevertheless, there are also reliable reports of the apparitions of the dead having indeed traveled and appeared to several people in various locations. Those, however, are not ghosts in the sense I understand the term. They are free spirits, or discarnate entities, who are inhabiting what Dr. Joseph B. Rhine of Duke University has called the "world of the mind." They may be attracted for emotional reasons to one or the other place at a given moment in order to communicate with someone on the earth plane. But a true ghost is unable to make such moves freely. Ghosts by their very nature are not unlike psychotics in the flesh; they are quite unable to understand fully their own predicament. They are kept in place, both in time and space, *by* their emotional ties to the spot. Nothing can pry them loose from it so long as they are reliving over and over again in their minds the events leading to their unhappy deaths.

Very few parapsychologists do anything about these trapped souls. I nearly always do, because I feel it my moral duty to help them out of their predicament, not just study their cases. The method I have developed over the years calls for the presence of a professional trance medium—that is a person who has the ability of slipping in and out of his or her physical body at times. This permits the ghost personality to use the medium's body to express himself.

When the ghost tells his tale of woe, he also relieves the pressure of being trapped in the spot of the haunting. It is a little like psychoanalysis except that the "patient" is not on a visible couch.

As soon as the identity of the haunting personality has been established through questioning by me, the ghost is coaxed into telling of his grievances. Gradually, I explain the true situation to him, that time has passed, that the matter no longer carries as much weight as it once did, and finally, gently, that he himself is "dead," though very much alive in another dimension, and should go out into it of his own free will.

Sometimes this is difficult for the ghost, as he may be too strongly attached to feelings of guilt or revenge to "let go." But eventually a combination of informative remarks by the parapsychologist and suggestions to call upon the deceased person's family will pry him loose and send him out into the free world of spirit.

Not many individuals have the proper ability or training to be good trance mediums. I have worked with Ethel Johnson Meyers, Sybil Leek, Betty Ritter, Trixie Allingham, and a few others, and I am constantly training young people in this very difficult branch of true mediumship.

The proof of superior mediumship lies only in the results. If the alleged ghost, while possessing the medium's body, can give substantial information about his past, and if that information is checked out by me and found to be substantially correct, then the "channel of communication" has been a good one.

In the majority of published cases, I have been able to prove that the knowledge obtained through a trance medium under my direction was unknown to the psychic person and could not have been obtained except by a qualified researcher such as myself, and even then with considerable effort.

Specific names, dates and situations concerning the life of the ghost have been brought to me in this manner, and there is no doubt in my mind that the information emanated from the so-called ghost. The best mediums serve simply as channels without expressing or even holding explanatory views of their skills, leaving that to the parapsychologist.

Ghosts have never harmed anyone except through fear found within the witness, of his own doing and because of his own ignorance as to what ghosts represent. In the few cases where ghosts have attacked people of flesh and blood, such as the ghostly abbot of Trondheim, it is simply a matter of mistaken identity, where extreme violence at the time of death has left a strong residue of memory in the individual ghost. By and large, it is entirely safe to be a ghost hunter, or to become a witness to phenomena of this kind.

In terms of physics, ghosts are electromagnetic fields originally encased in an outer layer called the physical body. At the time of death, that outer layer is dissolved, leaving the inner self free. With the majority of people, this inner self —also referred to as the soul by the church, or the psyche by others—will drift out into the nonphysical world where it is able to move forward or backward in time and space, being motivated by thought and possessed of all earth memories fully intact. Such a free spirit is indeed a development upward, and as rational a human being as he or she was on earth.

Not so with the ghost individual. Here the electromagnetic field is unable to move out into the wider reaches of the nonphysical world, but instead stays captive within the narrow confines of its earthly emotional entanglements. Nevertheless, it is of exactly the same nature as the personality field of those who do not have such problems. It can, therefore, be photographed, measured as an existing electric charge in the atmosphere, and otherwise dealt with by scientific means.

Science has long realized that all life energies are electric in nature. In my view, human personality is also made up of such energy particles. They are put together differently with each individual, resulting in the great variety of human character, but they are all working the same way—as carriers of personality, thoughts, feelings, and expressions.

Electrical impulses are capable of being recorded and measured. The "presence" of ghosts has already been proven with equipment designed along Geiger-counter lines. But I have always wanted to go one step further and prove these beings pictorially. Psychic photography is the answer. Ever since ordinary wet plates were invented and cameras used, there has also been an interest in photographing the Unseen.

Briefly, the system requires not only a camera and film, or at least light-sensitive photographic paper, but more importantly, the presence in the immediate vicinity of a person with the gift of photographic mediumship. Such an individual is able to act as catalyst between the thought-projection originating in the mind of the spirit or ghost and the light-sensitive film or paper. There is, in my view, some substance in the body of such a medium that makes the process of psychic photography possible. Certain glands secrete this substance only when the medium is "in operating condition," so to speak. I have worked with John Myers, Dr. Von Salza, Ethel Meyers, Betty Ritter—and other gifted individuals in this specific field. I myself have on occasion been able to get psychic photographs when there was someone with that special talent in my vicinity. The light-sensitive surface of film or paper seems to become coated with invisible but very sensitive psychic matter which, in turn, is capable of recording thought imprints from beyond the world of matter.

Naturally, all ordinary explanations must always be taken into consideration. Faulty equipment, light leaks, double exposure, faulty development or printing, reflections, refractions, and, finally, delusions of the viewer are all possible. Two examples of my own results are herewith reproduced to illustrate the point. After all the above-mentioned possible explanations had been weighed and

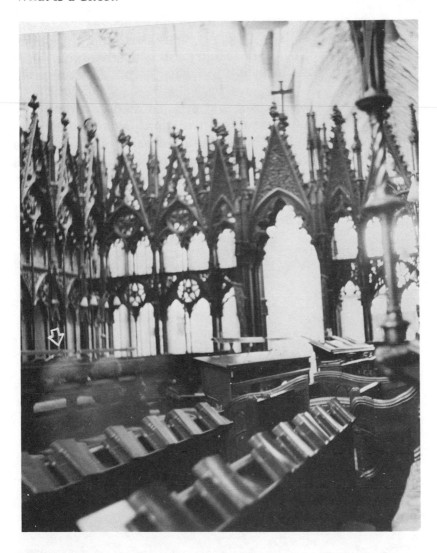

found to be unsatisfactory, only the parapsychological version remained.

Both photographs were taken by me with a perfect Zeiss camera, called the Super Ikonta B, with fresh Agfa Record Isopan film, and on firm surfaces. Both are time exposures of about two seconds, and the development and printing were done by first-rate people.

In the case of the three cowled monks seen at Winchester Cathedral, (see page 17), there is a history of persecutions during the reign of Henry VIII. Ghostly monks have from time to time been observed in the nave of the great church.

In the second case, that of a haunted house in Hollywood, California, a teen-ager was murdered during a wild party not too long ago, and disturbances have plagued the owners ever since. A partially visible figure slightly above the bed, dubbed by me "the girl in the negligee," cannot be accounted for by any "ordinary" explanation, such as window curtains, light reflection, and so on.

As for the photographs of actual ghosts, I have published them in *Psychic Photography-Threshold of a New Science*, and others elsewhere have also come forward with photographs taken in so-called haunted houses under conditions excluding fraud, double exposure, faulty equipment or development, and any other alternate explanation. Among these are a recent photograph taken at Newby Church in Yorkshire, England, revealing a cowled figure of a monk standing to the right of the altar. The picture clearly shows a semi-transparent figure with a whitish face and two holes for eyes but no recognizable features. In this particular instance, the photograph has been attested by an English photographic laboratory. The fact that photographs can be produced artificially to duplicate what has transpired under test conditions free of fakery does in no way affect the genuine facts. One must never forget that the possibility of fakery is not the same as the certainty of falsehood. It merely means that the expert must be fully aware of the possibilities and must devise his test conditions in such a way as to exclude any and all fraud. This has been done in all cases of ghost photographs published my me, and with such other authenticated pictures as the Newby church ghost monk, and the celebrated "lady on the staircase"—actually the brown lady of Raynham Hall, Yorkshire, England, which *Country Gentleman* and *Life* published in 1937.

In his chapter on ghosts, Douglas Hill, in *Man, Myth, and Magic*, takes all alternate hypotheses one by one and examines them. Having done so, he states, "None of these explanations is wholly satisfactory, for none seems applicable to the whole range of ghost lore." Try as man might, ghosts can't be explained away, nor will they disappear. They continue to appear frequently all over the world, to young and old, rich and poor, in old houses and in new houses, in airports and in streets, and wherever tragedy strikes man. For ghosts are indeed nothing more or nothing less than human beings trapped by special circumstances in this world while already being of the next. Or, to put it another way, human beings whose spirits are unable to leave the earthly surroundings because of unfinished business or emotional entanglements.

Ghosts, then, are very real, and the range of those who may at one time or another observe them is wide indeed. Anyone who sees or hears a ghostly phenomenon is by that very fact psychic. You do not have to be a professional medium to see a ghost, but you do have to be possessed of more than average ESP abilities to tune in on the refined "vibrations" or electromagnetic field that the human personality represents after it leaves the physical body. There are of course millions of such people in the world today, most of them not even aware of their particular talent.

This book lists some of the most interesting and most accessible haunted houses. These are houses where ghosts have been observed by one or more competent observers and where the likelihood of a re-occurrence of the phenomena still exists. There is no telling whether a casual visitor might have an experience or not. Ghosts do not appear on command, and even spending the night in a haunted house might produce nothing more than a stiff neck or the sniffles. Then again, one might walk into a haunted house, unaware of that fact, and have an experience quite unexpectedly. Such is the thrill, and the uncertainty, of following in a ghost hunter's footsteps—one can never be sure what might transpire.

In seeking out some of the houses described in the following pages, keep in mind that a relaxed, open-minded attitude toward the phenomena is helpful. Patience is a must. What might not happen on the first visit might very well occur on a subsequent trip. There is no hard and fast rule concerning the success one seeks in having a ghostly experience. There is only a reasonable likelihood of experiencing something in a haunted house if one is oneself somewhat psychic. If one is actually psychic to a high degree, then the chances are that one will at least feel something of the unseen inhabitant of the place. Whenever this is possible, take photographs using black and white film and time exposure, and something that the naked eye does not see might very well show up on your film.

And if you who read these lines are a complete skeptic and consider visiting haunted houses just a lark, remember an old quotation of uncertain origin, "I don't believe in ghosts, but I'm sure as hell scared stiff of 'em!"

But even if you do not encounter ghosts or have a psychic experience in the houses described here, you will find them fascinating places. As an adventure in historical research, haunted houses have no equal.

II
Are There Such Things as "Living" Ghosts?

As my investigations of psychic phenomena mounted in number and importance, it became increasingly clear to me that ghosts and spirits and human beings all must have something in common: if a living person can turn into a "dead" spirit or ghost, then that which survives must already have been contained within mortal man. We are as much spirit in our lifetime as we'll ever be.

I also noticed an amazing analogy between certain sleep and dream states and death—as reported by those claiming to be surviving entities speaking through entranced mediums.

The seat of personality seems encased within a temporary frame called the physical body. Under certain conditions, the personality (or soul, if you want to be religious-minded) can emerge from the "box" and behave independently of it. This is called astral travel, or out-of-the body experience. Here the separation is temporary and still under the control of the traveler—the sleeper. At death the separation is permanent and the personality, the inner self, leaves the "box" behind, rising to a new and freer existence in what Dr. Joseph Rhine of Duke University has called the world of the mind and what I prefer calling the non-physical world.

But there are cases where a ghost appears and on checking it is found that the one whose ghost it is is still alive and kicking.

Are there such things as "living ghosts"?

In 1920 Mrs. L. lived in a small oil town in Oklahoma. Her husband was a drilling contractor and their lives were ordinary lives without a trace of the uncanny. One morning Mrs. L. awoke to the sound of a buzzer that preceded the sounding of the hour on her alarm clock. She opened her eyes and noticed it was 7 A.M., or rather five minutes before the hour. In direct line between her eyes and the wall was a chest of drawers. Between the chest and the window there was some space, and as her eyes fastened themselves on that area, she became aware of a figure standing there. It was her husband, staring straight at her. However, she noticed that the apparition ended at the knees where the figure faded out. He wore his usual tan pants, but she also noticed a white shirt with purple stripes. What puzzled her about this shirt was the fact that it was at this moment neatly tucked away inside the chest of drawers.

Now the figure of her husband started to fade away, slowly, from the bottom on up. By the time the apparition had fully dissolved, the clock chimed the hour—seven o'clock.

Mrs. L. got up quickly and opened the chest of drawers; there was the shirt. Before she realized what she was doing, she had torn the shirt to bits!

A short time after, Mr. L. was involved in an explosion at the oil rig where he worked. He was blown into a wheelhouse and knocked unconscious. Everything around him was on fire, but he came to just in time to grab a plank and kick it out of the wheelhouse, and thus make his escape.

At the time she saw her husband's "ghost," Mrs. L. was sure he was alive. She was equally convinced that it was a kind of warning. If she hadn't destroyed the telltale shirt and if he had worn it that fatal day, would he have been able to save himself?

A tantalizing question.

"Haven't seen a ghost now for about two years," confided the lady from New Britain, Connecticut, who had come to hear my lecture at the college.

It turned out she had seen ghosts galore before that date, however. Mrs. Lillian Dorval had a husband, a daughter, and a lot of common sense. But she is very psychic, like it or not.

The first time anything unusual happened was in 1957. She had just fed the baby her bottle and fallen asleep, around midnight. Suddenly she awoke to see what she thought was her husband standing beside her bed. It was 2 A.M. When she asked him what he was doing, standing there like that, he did not answer. So Mrs. Dorval reached over and switched on the light. There in bed beside her was her husband, sleeping peacefully.

When she explained that she had just seen him standing near her bed, he thought she had had a nightmare. But she had no doubt about it—she knew she had been awake. What she did not know at the time was that she had just undergone an experience of bi-location. Mrs. Dorval encountered the "living ghosts" again, some time after her husband had passed away unexpectedly. A friend of hers had left her and she had gone to bed. In the middle of the night she saw his apparition standing by her bed. He was very much alive at the moment she saw him, perhaps still thinking of their evening together.

In November, 1966, she saw an apparition of a man she could not recognize at the time. Again it was in the very heart of the night, around 1 A.M.

Several months later she met this man and became friendly with him. Obviously he had been alive at the time she saw his apparition—but how could one explain this link, since she had not yet encountered him, nor he her, except by prevision on her part.

"Regular" ghosts—that is, of dead people—are nothing new to her, of course.

Take her favorite Uncle Harry, for instance. Five days after the family had buried him, there he stood on the right side of her bed. All the "living ghosts," projections of people still in the body, had always appeared on her *left* side. Moreover, the living ones were in color while Uncle Harry wore a plain white suit. When she switched the lights on, he melted away like the others.

Mrs. Dorval fears ridicule so she has not seen fit to talk about her experiences. She also has had out-of-the-body experiences of her own when she found herself soaring out onto rooftops and trees. And the incident she remembers most vividly was her neighbor's funeral, which she attended. While the proceedings went forward in the customary manner, she noticed the neighbor sitting on a wall near the casket, laughing and looking over the mourners.

Projections of living people, or "Phantasms of the Living," as the author Sidgwick has called them, occur when people's thoughts are so strongly engaged at a distance that part of their personality travels with them. If the person on the other end of the "line" happens to be receptive, that is, a psychic person "in tune" with the sender, reception of an image or even a voice may result. And yet, by nature, the ghosts of the living and the ghosts of the dead have much in ccommon. Both prove by the sheer weight of the evidence——numerous as these cases are—that man possesses an indestructible inner self which is capable of breaking through the conventional limits of time and space.

III
How to Live with a Poltergeist

A far cry from the fantasies of an 'Amityville Horror', an average American family has learned to live with the 'lively dead' in their old farmhouse.

Despite horror movies and exaggerated stories bandied about, the reality of being in the very center of an ongoing haunting is quite different.

"The first time I walked into this house, I felt something horrible had happened in it," says Nancy Jones, housewife and mother of three children aged 7, 4, and 2—"but I thought it was my imagination at first."

The Jones moved into the old farm house near a small New Jersey town back in the summer of 1975. Tom Jones had been a captain in the Air Force when he and Nancy met in her native Little Rock, Arkansas. This was his father's former home, and he had promised to restore it to its former glory, if possible. The task seemed formidable enough: the woods around it had to be cleared with bulldozers so they could do some farming again, every window in the house was broken, screens were missing, and filth was on every one of the three floors. Tom left the Air Force where he had been a pilot and settled down to married life as a supervisor for a large food processing company. He was going to do most of the restoration work in the house himself, but soon realized he did need professional help, so a succession of carpenters and paperhangers were brought in to lend a hand. They rebuilt the third floor, making many structural changes, perhaps inadvertantly setting off something of the uncanny. The day the Jones moved in, Leslie Anne was 3, little September was six months old, and Thomas Morgan hadn't been born as yet.

Soon, Nancy Jones had forgotten all about her initial apprehension on moving into the old house.

"About four weeks afterwards, I was alone in the house, I had just put the children to bed—when I heard children *laughing outside*. I was standing in the downstairs dining room at the time, so I ran outside to look—there were no children outside. I ran upstairs and found the kids in bed taking their afternoon nap."

That summer, Nancy heard the invisible children several times more—always when her own were safely in bed. Finally, they decided to call in their friend Lois, who had some knowledge of psychic matters, because the Jones were beginning to wonder about the house. Their discomfort was greatly increased when she discovered her daughter Leslie Anne, then age 3 and a half, in lively conversation with an unseen 'friend'. The Jones weren't particularly worried about "ghosts." They had always had an open mind about life after death, and it was merely a matter of curiosity to them, to find out if they shared their house with something —or someone—from the past who hadn't quite left it.

"We decided to hold a little séance in the front parlor," Tom Jones explained," and we were trying to talk this thing with the unseen children out once and for all. But all of a sudden Lois started to talk like the children, conversing with an unknown child in a very high-pitched, childish tone . . . they were talking about playing *outside* . . . it was rather entertaining, nothing at all fearful . . . and after that séance, the phenomenon of the unseen children disappeared . . . except for the gravestone."

I had been listening with silent interest, but now my ears perked up. I had seen the gravestone in back of the house.

"We found the gravestone when we cleared the land," Tom Jones continued, "and had to move it periodically to get it out of the way, finally leaving it in the field about a hundred yards away from the house. But after our little séance, all of a sudden it just decided to locate itself right outside our back door."

The Jones had tried to find the grave site, but without success. The stone marked the grave of two children, aged 13 and seven weeks, who had died in 1891 and 1889 respectively, but had for some unknown reason been placed under the same stone. The children had been part of the family that had built the house in the last century.

"Funny thing is, it would have taken four strong men to move that gravestone . . . and none of us did it. Happened the day after we held that memorial séance."

The Jones figured the children were now at rest, but they soon discovered their house wasn't.

About a year later, Nancy was walking up the stairs to the second floor where the master bedroom is located, when she saw a tall, slender man standing 'over' her bed!

"He and I realized instantly that we had caught each other, and he began to disintegrate before my eyes from the top on down."

A little later, the Jones' eldest girl Leslie Anne began 'falling' out of her bed—eventually winding up on the far side of her room. What or who had put her there, the Jones wondered. Two days after the last 'fall', the little girl came down to breakfast and asked if her mother had come up to check on her the night before.

"Because . . . this lady with the pretty, long blond hair and a white dress came to see me . . . and she asked me to go with her . . . and I told her I couldn't go with somebody I didn't know, I had to ask my Mom and she said she'd come back . . ."

"How did you explain *that* to the little girl?" I wondered out loud. "I think we discussed angels rather vaguely and let it go at that," Nancy Jones replied, "but our children are brought up to accept life after death, so she wasn't upset."

As if the man disintegrating in her bedroom and the blond lady weren't enough extra population, Nancy also noticed some "white spots on the wall" in the bedroom—she has the uncanny feeling that Ella Hauser, the woman who built their house, was still around checking up on them.

Tom Jones is a man with a practical, down-to-earth outlook, despite his experiences with the uncanny. But the situation involving his tools was too much even for him.

"I was working with sheet rock, and I used a very heavy flat-headed hammer. I left it up on the third floor at night, but when I went up there early next morning, the hammer was gone. Finally, I found it tucked into little crevices in the wall. Then my nails started to disappear. Then my sheet rock knife."

"And where did you find them afterwards?"

"Under things that I know I couldn't have put them under . . . it felt like somebody didn't want me to finish that attic . . . the job should have taken six weeks. It took me about four months, with all those interruptions."

But the Jones weren't alone in their encounters with the unknown. A baby sitter also named Nancy had just put the two girls to bed, back in August of 1977, and all the kids were up there on the third floor. All of a sudden Nancy heard someone going through the drawers downstairs.

"She thought maybe someone was opening and closing the drawers looking for something, and her first thought was, it's Prudence the cat doing it," Mrs. Jones said. "But then she rocked the baby a little more, and underneath the rocker, there was the cat. When she came downstairs nothing had been touched."

That was one baby sitter lost to the Jones. Nothing would get her to go back to "that house" again.

About that time there had been a number of robberies in the area, so it was natural for Nancy Jones to think they had a prowler in the house the night she went downstairs for a drink and found a five-foot ten-inches tall man standing in her living room, at three in the morning!

"I was so scared when I saw his black belt buckle, and one of those khaki shirts farmers wear, and a pair of brown work pants . . . everything was too big for the guy, I could tell it was an old man . . . I took one look and ran upstairs. I told my husband; he said, let's wait."

I seemed perplexed by that, so Tom added—"You see, he might have had a gun. I didn't. We had agreed that if the prowler came to the top of the stairs, we would defend ourselves and the children . . . we had a baseball bat in the closet . . . but hopefully, since he had been observed, he would leave. . . ."

There is quite a bit of silver downstairs, and some valuable paintings. The Jones have good taste.

What about the prowler?

"He was as solid as you are," Nancy said, "I couldn't see *through him* like the other one . . . he seemed like a real, live human being standing in my living room at three o'clock in the morning, with the house locked up tight."

"We went down the next morning," Tom Jones continued. "Nothing had been touched. Even the dust was intact on every window sill. Doors and windows still locked. Basement door locked. There was no way *a man* could have gotten in or out."

By that time the Jones felt they needed some professional advice, so they got in touch with me. They had read some of my books and thought I could supply some answers to the puzzle. I agreed to have a look. While they were waiting for me, the phenomena moved into their kitchen.

"Three weeks ago I came in late one night, and I saw what appeared to be some kind of fog in our kitchen," Nancy reported, "a strange haze all over the top of the room. We have a Fisher stove in the kitchen but it hadn't been lit that evening."

Nancy realized that some unseen force or person was giving her the once-over, especially as they were constantly changing things around in the house, trying to make it as comfortable to their own taste as they could.

"One day I'm in the kitchen, and I am about to put a glass on the second shelf, and the next thing I know the glass falls out of the shelf, goes all the way into the back of the bottom shelf and breaks three other glasses inside. In plain daylight."

"What did you do?"

"I screamed, Leave my glasses alone! I couldn't afford it. You've got to deal with this sort of thing, and it backs off . . ."

"Is it still around . . . I mean, *them*?"

Nancy Jones nodded emphatically.

"They must have known you were coming . . . the last thing was this morning in the loft. Tom comes home early in the morning, working the night shift. The door is always locked. Today I wanted to surprise him, so I *unlocked* the door, just so I could see the surprise on his face when he comes in. But when he came home five minutes later, the door was locked tight. *I didn't lock that door.*"

I've met thousands of people who have problems with ghosts. Some are frightened, some laugh at it and try to ignore it, some exaggerate their problems into Amityville horror-type stories—and some come to terms with it, like the Jones.

"I've gone from thinking it was funny to not thinking it was funny to being traumatized to total frustration and back to thinking it was funny, to learning to live with it . . . I've made my peace with *her*. I'd like her to leave, because it's my house. The old saying is true, you cannot put two women in one house. It's my house, it's not hers anymore."

I wondered how the neighbors felt about the house, the Jones . . . and *them*.

"Oh, we're known as the nuts that live down the road," Nancy shrugged," of course I'm tired of being laughed at, so I won't talk about it anymore."

"I can't deny that these things happened," Tom added calmly, "they did. I don't get excited about them. I've dealt with the trauma, it's just another assignment to me. But I ask myself, why all of a sudden so many revelations about life after death and reincarnation? Surely, our situation is far from unique. Maybe contemporary religion is out of focus with what's really happening?"

"Do you discuss it with people at work?"

"You don't bring it up in open conversation . . . you find a common denominator and pretty soon you bring out from various people incidents that they can't explain. . . ."

How did he feel about Ella, who built the house and was loathe to leave it, even in death?

Tom Jones thought about my question for a moment.

"Ella and I get along fine, because I can go to bed at night and not feel bothered. I walk in, Ella you got your space, I've got mine. Just don't bother the kids, don't bother our lifestyle, we've got work to do."

The Jones have read the best-selling *Amityville Horror*. They enjoy an entertaining thriller. But they know what it's like to live with ghosts *first-hand*.

IV
Public Houses, America

1

**The Whaley House
California.**

There are many old houses in southern California, some going back to the Spanish period. Quite a number of them have had ghostly manifestations. But none were as spectacular and as manifold and received as much notice as the manifestations at the Whaley House in San Diego, in a part called Old Town; a house going back only to 1857, but of great importance both historically and to ghost hunters because of the well-documented incidents which have occurred there and which are, as a matter of fact, still occurring. There is no reason to doubt that one or the other of the very active ghosts are still about the house.

The Whaley House was originally built in 1857 as a two-storied mansion for a certain Thomas Whaley, one of the early pioneers of the city of San Diego, California. The house stands at the corner of San Diego Avenue and Harney Street and is nowadays kept up as a museum under the direction of Mrs. June Reading. Visitors are admitted during daylight hours and there are usually a lot of them as the fame of the house has spread throughout the United States.

There are two stories connected by a staircase. Downstairs there is a parlor, a music room, a library, and in the annex, to the left of the entrance, there used to be the County Courthouse. At least one of the hauntings is connected with the courtroom. Upstairs there are four bedrooms, tastefully furnished in the period during which the Whaley House was at its zenith—that is to say, between 1860 and 1890. The house was restored by a group of history-minded citizens in 1956.

Numerous witnesses, both visitors to the house and those serving as part-time guides or volunteers, have seen ghosts here. These include the figure of a woman in the courtroom, sounds of footsteps in various parts of the house, windows opening by themselves in the upper part of the house, (despite the fact that strong bolts had been installed and thus they could only be opened by someone on the inside); the figure of a man in a frock coat and pantaloons standing at the top of the stairs, organ music being played in the courtroom (where there is, in fact, an organ although at the time no one was near it and the cover was closed), even a ghost dog has been seen scurrying down the hall toward the dining room.

There is a black rocking chair upstairs that moves of its own volition at times, as if someone were sitting in it. A woman dressed in a green plaid gingham dress has been seen in one of the bedrooms upstairs. Smells include perfume and cigars. There is also a child ghost present, which has been observed by a number of people working in the house, and a baby has been heard crying. Strange lights, cool breezes, and cold spots have added to the general atmosphere of haunting permeating the entire house. It is probably one of the most actively haunted mansions in the world today.

The ghosts include the builder of the house, Thomas Whaley, who had a just grievance against the city of San Diego, which probably has kept him tied to the house. He had put money into certain alterations so that he could sell the house to the county to be used as a courthouse. However, his contract was never executed and he was left "holding the bag." Sybil Leek pinpointed a child ghost, age twelve, by the name of Annabelle, and she also named the lady ghost upstairs correctly as Anna Lannay, Thomas Whaley's wife!

It is wise to ask for a guided tour, or at the very least check in with Mrs. June Reading to be sure that the ghostly spots are properly pointed out. Since there are so many of them, one can hardly avoid at least one of the several hauntings at the Whaley House.

There may be an even older ghost on the premises dating to the time when the spot was used to court-martial a criminal who was hanged as a result. At that time, Russian sailors came to San Diego as part of their whaling expeditions and this was truly the Wild West.

Whatever the ghostly manifestations a visitor might still feel or even encounter, none of them are dangerous in the least, and there is no need to worry about any horrible experiences. The ghosts at Disneyland are more frightful.

2

The Ghostly Stagecoach Inn
Thousand Oaks, California

Not far from Ventura, at Thousand Oaks, a few yards back from the main road, stands an old stagecoach inn, now run as a museum; between 1952 and 1965, while in the process of being restored to its original appearance, it also served as a gift shop under the direction of a Mr. and Mrs. MacIntyre who had sensed the presence of a female ghost in the structure.

The house has 19 rooms and an imposing frontage with columns running from the floor to the roof. There is a balcony in the central portion, and all windows have shutters, in the manner of the middle nineteenth century. Surrounded by trees until a few years ago, it has been moved recently to a new position to make room for the main road running through here. Nevertheless, its grandeur has not been affected by the move.

During the stagecoach days, bandits were active in this area. The inn had been erected because of the Butterfield Mail route, which was to have gone through the Conejo Valley on the way to St. Louis. The Civil War halted this plan, and the routing was changed to go through the Santa Clara Valley.

I investigated the stagecoach inn with Mrs. Gwen Hinzie and Sybil Leek. Up the stairs to the left of the staircase Sybil noticed one of the particularly haunted rooms. She felt that a man named Pierre Devon was somehow connected with the building. Since the structure was still in a state of disrepair, with building activities going on all around us, the task of walking up the stairs was not only a difficult one but also somewhat dangerous, for we could not be sure that the wooden structure would not collapse from our weight. We stepped very gingerly. Sybil seemed to know just where to turn as if she had been there before. Eventually, we would up in a little room to the left of the stairwell. It must have been one of the smaller rooms, a "single" in today's terms.

Sybil complained of being cold all over. The man, Pierre Devon, had been killed in that room, she insisted, sometime between 1882 and 1889.

She did not connect with the female ghost. However, several people living in the area have reported the presence of a tall stranger who could only be seen out of the corner of an eye, never for long. Pungent odors, perfume of a particularly heavy kind, also seem to waft in and out of the structure.

Like inns in general, this one may have more undiscovered ghosts hanging on to the spot. Life in nineteenth-century wayside inns did not compare favorably with life in today's Hilton. Some people going to these stagecoach inns for a night's rest never woke up to see another day.

Thousand Oaks is about an hour and a half from Los Angeles on the Ventura Freeway. No special permission to visit is needed.

3

The Haunted Organ
at Yale University
New Haven, Connecticut

Yale University in New Haven, Connecticut is an austere and respectable institution, not taking such matters as ghostly manifestations very lightly. I must therefore keep the identity of my informant a secret, but anyone who wishes to visit Yale and admire its magnificent historical organ is, of course, at liberty to do so, provided he or she gets clearance from the proper authorities. I would suggest, however, that the matter of ghostly goings-on not be mentioned at such a time. If you happen to experience something out of the ordinary while visiting the organ, well and good, but let it not be given as the reason to the university authorities for your intended visit.

I first heard about this unusual organ in 1969 when a gentleman who was then employed as an assistant at Yale had been asked to look after the condition and possible repairs of the huge organ, a very large instrument located in Woolsey Hall. This is the fifth largest organ in the world and has a most interesting history.

Woolsey Hall was built as part of a complex of three buildings for Yale's two hundredth anniversary in 1901 by the celebrated architects, Carere and Hastings. Shortly after its completion the then university organist, Mr. Harry B. Jepson, succeeded in getting the Newberry family, of the famous department store clan, to contribute a large sum of money for a truly noble organ to be built for the hall.

Even in 1903 it was considered to be an outstanding instrument because of its size and range. By 1915, certain advances in the technology of pipe organs made the 1903 instruments somewhat old fashioned. Again Jepson contacted the Newberry family about the possibility of updating their gift so that the organ could be rebuilt and the hall enlarged. This new instrument was then dedicated in 1916 or thereabouts.

By 1926, musical tastes had again changed further toward romantic music and it became necessary to make certain additions to the stops as well as the basic building blocks of the classical ensemble. Once again the Newberry family contributed toward the updating of the instrument. The alterations were undertaken by the Skinner Organ Company of Boston, in conjunction with an English expert by the name of G. Donald Harrison. Skinner and Harrison did not get on well together and much tension was present when they restored and brought up to date the venerable old organ.

Professor Harry Jepson was forced to retire in the 1940s, against his wishes, and though he lived down the street only two blocks from Woolsey Hall, he never set foot again into it to play the famous organ which he had caused to be built. He died a bitter and disappointed man sometime in 1952.

The last university organist, Frank Bozyan, retired in the 1970s, with great misgivings. He confided to someone employed by the hall that he felt he was making a mistake; within six months after his retirement he was dead. As time went on, Woolsey Hall, once a temple of beauty in the fine arts, was being used for youth programs involving rock and roll groups and mechanically amplified music. Undoubtedly, those connected with the building of the hall and the organ would have been horrified at the goings-on, had they been able to witness them.

A gentleman who brought all of this to my attention and who shall remain nameless, had occasion to be in the hall and involved with the organ itself on many a day. He became aware of a menacing and melancholic sensation in the entire building, particularly in the basement and the organ chambers. While working there at odd hours late in the night, he became acutely aware of some sort of unpleasant sensation just lurking around the next corner or even standing behind him! On many occasions he found it necessary to look behind him in order to make sure he was alone. The feeling of a presence became so strong he refused to be there by himself, especially in the evenings. Allegedly, the wife of one of the curators advised him to bring a crucifix whenever he had occasion to go down to the organ chambers. She also claimed to have felt someone standing at the entrance door to the basement, as if to keep strangers out.

I visited Yale and the organ one fine summer evening in the company of my informant, who has since then found employment elsewhere. I, too, felt the oppressive air in the organ chambers, the sense of a presence whenever I moved about. Whether we are dealing here with the ghost of the unhappy man who was forced to retire and never set foot again into his beloved organ chamber, or whether we are dealing with an earlier influence, is hard to say. Not for a minute do I suggest that Yale University is haunted or that there are any evil influences concerning the university itself. But it is just possible that sensitive individuals visiting the magnificent organ at Woolsey Hall might pick up some remnant of an unresolved past.

4

John Wilkes Booth's Tavern
Clinton, Maryland

A number of people have seen Abraham Lincoln's ghost walk the corridors of the White House, and others have reported unusual experiences at Ford's Theatre in Washington, where the actor John Wilkes Booth shot President Lincoln. Less known is an historical tavern in what is now Clinton, Maryland.

Thirteen miles south of Washington, in a small town now called Clinton but once known as Surrattville, stands an eighteenth-century building nowadays used as a museum. Mary Surratt ran it as an inn at the time when the area was far enough removed from Washington to serve as a way station to those travelling south from the nation's capital. When business fell off, however, Mrs. Surratt leased the eighteenth-century tavern to John Lloyd and moved to Washington where she ran a boardinghouse on H Street between Sixth and Seventh Streets. But she remained on close and friendly relations with her successor at the tavern at Surrattville, so that it was possible for her son, John Surratt, to use it as an occasional meeting place with his friends. These friends included John Wilkes Booth, and the meetings eventually led to the plot to assassinate President Lincoln.

After the murder, Booth escaped on horseback and made straight for the tavern. By prearrangement, he and an associate hid the guns they had with them in a cache in the floor of the tavern. Shortly after, he and the associate, David Herald, split up, and John Wilkes Booth continued his journey despite a broken foot. Eventually, he was discovered hiding at Garrett's barn and was shot there.

The connection between Booth and the tavern was no longer public knowledge as the years went by. Some local people might have remembered it, but the outside world had lost interest. At one time, it appears, the structure was acquired by John's brother, the actor Edwin Booth. In the 1950s it passed into the hands of a local businessman named B. K. Miller. By now the village was known as Clinton, since the Surrattville name had been changed shortly after the infamous trial of Mary Surratt.

The hauntings observed here include the figure of a woman thought to be the restless spirit of Mary Surratt herself, whose home this had been at one time. Strange men have been observed sitting on the back stairs when there was no one but the occupants of the house around. Muffled voices of a group of men talking in excited tones have also been reported, and seem to indicate that at the very least an imprint from the past has been preserved at the Surratt Tavern. Many meetings of the conspirators had taken place in the downstairs part of the building, and when I brought Sybil Leek to the tavern she immediately pointed out the site of the meetings, the place where the guns had been hidden, and, in trance, established communication with the former owner of the tavern, Edwin Booth himself.

Although the building is now a museum and open to visitors, one should first obtain permission from Mr. Miller, at Miller's Supermarket, in Clinton, Maryland. Clinton itself is less than an hour's drive from downtown Washington. As far as I know there is no fee attached to a visit at Surratt Tavern. At the time when I made my investigation, Mr. Miller had thought of selling the building to a museum or an historical trust, and by the time this appears in print, it may well have changed hands.

Anyone who is psychic and visits the old tavern might very well hear the same voices, or have some kind of psychic experience because the phenomena themselves have not faded away, nor are they likely to, since no formal exorcism has ever been attempted there.

5

The Ghosts at the
Ship Chandlery,
Massachusetts

Moving an old house from its original location to a new spot frequently awakens the ghostly manifestations which may have been slumbering in it for a long time. Such was the case when the Historical Society of Cohasset, Massachusetts, moved the old ship's chandlery inland somewhat for the sake of convenience so that more tourists could visit it. Cohassett is about an hour's drive from Boston, a very old town which used to make its living mainly from the sea.

When we arrived at the wooden structure on a corner of the post Road—it had a nautical look, its two stories squarely set down as if to withstand any gale—we found several people already assembled. Among them were Mrs. E. Stoddard Marsh, the curator of the Museum, which is what the Ship's Chandlery now is, and her associate, lean, quiet Robert Fraser. The others were friends and neighbors. We entered the building and walked around the downstairs portion, admiring its displays of nautical supplies ranging from fishing tackle and scrim-shaw made from walrus teeth, to heavy anchors, hoists and rudders—all the instruments and wares of a shipchandler's business.

Built in the late eighteenth century by Samuel Bates, the building was owned by the Bates family, notably by one John Bates, second of the family to have the place, who had died seventy-eight years before our visit. Something of a local character, John Bates had cut a swath around the area as a gay blade. He could well afford the role, for he owned a fishing fleet of twenty-four vessels and business was good in those far-off days when the New England coast was dotted with major ports for fishing and shipping. A handwritten record of his daily catch can be seen next to a mysterious closet full of ladies' clothes. Mr. Bates led a full life.

I questioned Mrs. Marsh, the curator, about strange happenings in the house, especially after it was moved to its present site. "Two years ago we were having a lecture here. There were about 40 people listening to Francis Hagerty talk about old sailing boats. I was sitting over here to the left—on this ground floor—with Robert Fraser, when all of a sudden we heard heavy footsteps upstairs and things being moved and dragged—so I said to Mr. Fraser, 'Someone is up there; will you please tell him to be quiet'—I thought it was kids."

There was a man who had helped them with the work at the Museum who had lately stayed away for reasons unknown. Could he have heard the footsteps too and decided that caution was the better part of valor?

"The other day, just recently, four of us went into the room this gentleman occupies when he is here, and the *door closed on us* by itself. It had never done that before."

We decided to go upstairs now, and see If Mr. Bates—or whoever the ghost might be—felt like walking for us. We quietly waited in the semi-darkness upstairs, near the area where the footsteps had been heard, but nothing happened.

"The steps went back and forth," Mrs. Marsh reiterated, "heavy, masculine steps, the kind a big man would make."

A year after my visit to the Ship's Chandlery of Cohassett, nothing further was heard from the curators. Evidently, John Bates must have simmered down after all. If you happen to be up near Boston and feel like visiting the house at Cohassett, do so by all means. Maybe you will be luckier than I was, and John Bates will put in an appearance.

6

The Ocean-Born Mary House
New Hampshire

In one of the most beautiful parts of New Hampshire, there is a truly impressive New England mansion known nowadays as the Ocean-born Mary House, a name which has stuck to it ever since it was built by a certain Mary Wallace who was born aboard ship while crossing over to the New World. I have been to the Ocean-born Mary House several times and conducted three separate investigations there with

two different mediums, and the material was truly astounding. So were the eyewitness accounts of those who have seen a ghost in the house or at the window.

Nevertheless, because neighborhood youths kept making the house a target for their Halloween pranks, the owners began to shy away from the true story and eventually told eager tourists that there was nothing to the ghosts after all and to please not bother them. Thus, if you intend visiting the Ocean-born Mary House in Henniker, New Hampshire, about an hour's ride out of Boston, do so because you want to visit an historical mansion and do not bring up the matter of ghosts with the present owners.

Mary was the "ocean-born child" who was befriended by a pirate, named Don Pedro. Later in life he helped her build this house and in turn she permitted him to spend his old age there. Unfortunately for Don Pedro, so the story goes, one of his men who had been angry with him, caught up with him, and in the ensuing fight Don Pedro was killed. Allegedly, his body lies underneath the fireplace, but there is no proof since the fireplace has never been dug up.

The place came to my attention when a local amateur medium, Mrs. A., asked my assistance in dealing with the phenomena she had encountered at the house. During a routine visit as a tourist, she had found herself practically taken over by the spirit of Mary Wallace who demanded to be heard through her. Frightened, she fled home to a Boston suburb. That night she awoke and, without being able to resist, drove her car all the way up to New Hampshire, still in her nightclothes.

I brought Mrs. A. back to Ocean-born Mary's with me, in the daytime and wearing street clothes, and in trance Mary Wallace manifested. The gist of her communication through the medium was a concern for the proper maintenance of the old house and an almost playful desire to be acknowledged and recognized.

Subsequent to this visit I also drove up with Sybil Leek and attempted another trance session. Sybil managed to bring through a servant girl who had apparently met with

foul play or was involved in it. At any rate, she must be the
third resident ghost, in addition to Mary Wallace and her
pirate friend.

There was also talk of a buried treasure somewhere on
the grounds. The directions were quite explicit and after
Sybil came out of trance, we all went out and looked for the
treasure underneath the stones behind the house. We did not
dig, of course, and treasures have a way of staying underground, especially after 250 years.

While there may be some speculation about the reality
of the hidden treasure and possibly of the continued residence "in spirit" of the pirate, there is substantial evidence
that the house is haunted by a woman greatly resembling the
original owner.

A number of people have seen the tall, stately figure of
Mary Wallace peering out of an upstairs window of the
two-story structure. It was her favorite place, and from the
description given there is no doubt that those who saw the
figure were indeed seeing the ghost of Mary Wallace.

On one occasion, her intervention saved the house
from burning to the ground. A heater had caught fire, but was
smothered by unseen hands. The ghost has been described
by one who saw her as "a lovely lady in her thirties with
auburn-colored hair, smiling rather intensely and thought-
fully."

On another occasion, two state troopers saw her walking down the road leading up to the house, wearing a
Colonial-type costume, and a casual visitor to the house was
shown around by a tall lady at a time when the owners were
away. Only later did this visitor realize that it had been Mary
Wallace who had been so hospitable.

The house can be reached by car from Boston. It is
worth a visit. If you are wondering about the reality of pirates
in the late eighteenth century in this area, be assured that it
was not uncommon for such men of the sea to retire to their
beloved New England, to settle down at a safe distance from
the sea. There are other mansions and manor houses in the
area which owe their existence to the wealth accumulated by

sea captains, some of them of doubtful honesty, but nevertheless, if it weren't for them, these houses would have never been built. Thus, we do owe Don Pedro a debt of gratitude for having caused Mary Wallace to erect this beautiful New England mansion.

7

The "Spy House" Ghosts
New Jersey

In June, 1696, one Daniel Seabrook, aged 26 and a planter by profession, took his inheritance of 80 pounds sterling and bought 202 acres of property from his stepfather, Thomas Whitlock. For 250 years this plantation was in the hands of the Seabrook family who worked the land and sailed their ships from the harbor. The "Spy House" is probably one of the finest pieces of Colonial architecture available for inspection in the eastern United States, having been restored meticulously over the years.

The house is built in the old manner, held together with wooden pegs. There are handmade bricks, filled with clay mortar. The house has two stories and is painted white. Every room has its own fireplace as that was the only way in which Colonial houses could be heated.

Today, the house, which is located near Middletown, New Jersey, can easily be reached from New York City. It is being kept by a group headed by curator Gertrude Neidlinger, helped by her historian-brother, Travis Neidlinger, and as a museum it displays not only the furniture of the Colonial period but some of the implements of the whalers who were active in the area well into the nineteenth century. As an historical attraction, it is something that should not be missed by anyone, apart from any ghostly connections.

One of the rooms in the house is dedicated to the period of the Battle of Monmouth. This room, called the spy room by the British for good reasons, as we shall see, has copies of the documents kept in the Library of Congress in

Washington, D.C., which are among General Washington's private papers.

In 1778, the English were marching through Middletown, pillaging and burning the village. Along the shoreline the Monmouth militia and the men who were working the whale boats, got together to try to cut down the English shipping. General Washington asked for a patriot from Shoal Harbor, which was the name of the estate where the spy house is located, to help the American side fight the British. The volunteer was a certain Corporal John Stillwell, who was given a telescope and instructions to spy on the British from a hill called Garrett's Hill, not far away, the highest point in the immediate area.

The lines between British and Americans were intertwined and frequently intercut each other, and it was difficult for individuals to avoid crossing them at times. The assignment given Corporal Stillwell was not an easy one, especially as some of his own relatives favored the other side in the war. Still, he was able to send specific messages to the militia who were able to turn these messages into attacks on the British fleet.

At that point, Stillwell observed there were 1,037 vessels in the fleet lying off the New Jersey coastline, at a time when the American forces had no navy at all. But the fishermen and their helpers on shore did well in this phase of the Revolutionary War. John Stillwell's son, Obadiah Stillwell, 17 years old, served as message carrier from his father's observation point to the patriots.

Twenty-three naval battles were fought in the harbor after the battle of Monmouth. The success of the whaleboat operation was a stunning blow to the British fleet and a great embarrassment. Even daylight raids became so bold and successful that in one day two pilot boats were captured upsetting the harbor shipping.

Finally, the British gave the order to find the spy and end the rebel operation. The searching party declared the Seabrook homestead as a spy house, since they knew its owner, Major Seabrook, was a patriot. They did not realize that the real spy was John Stillwell, operating from Garrett's Hill. Nevertheless, they burned the spy house. It was, of course, later restored. Today, descendants of John Stillwell are among the society of friends of the museum, supporting it.

Gertrude Neidlinger turned to me for help with the several ghosts she felt in the house. Considering the history of the house, it is not surprising that there should be ghosts there. Miss Neidlinger, herself, has felt someone in the entrance room whenever she has been alone in the house, especially at night. There is also a lady in white who comes down from the attic, walks along the hall and goes into what is called the blue and white room, and there tucks in the covers of a crib or bed. Then she turns and goes out of sight. Miss Neidlinger was not sure who she was, but thought she might have been the spirit of Mrs. Seabrook, who lived through the Revolutionary War in a particularly dangerous position, having relatives on both sides of the political fence.

In 1976, I brought Ingrid Beckman, my psychic friend, to the spy house, which is technically located in Keansburg, New Jersey, near Middletown. The number on the house is 119, but of course everyone in the area calls it the Spy House. As Ingrid walked about the place, she immediately pointed out its ancient usage as an outpost. While we were investigating the house, we both clearly heard footsteps overhead where there was no one walking. Evidently, the ghosts knew of our arrival.

Without knowing anything about the history of the house, Ingrid commented, "Down here around the fireplace I feel there are people planning strategy, worried about British ships." Then she continued, "This was to mobilize something like the minutemen, farming men who were to fight. This was a strategic point because it was the entry into New York."

I then asked Ingrid to tell me whether she felt any ghosts, any residues of the past still in the house.

When we went upstairs, Ingrid tuned into the past with a bang. "There's a woman here. She ties in with this house and something about spying, some kind of spying went on here." Then she added, "Somebody spied behind the American lines and brought back information."

Upstairs near the window on the first floor landing, Ingrid felt a man watching, waiting for someone to come his way. Ingrid felt there was a man present who had committed an act of treason, a man who gave information back to the British. His name was Samuels. She felt that this man was hanged publicly. The people call him an ex-patriot. This is the entity, Ingrid said, who cannot leave this house out of remorse.

Ingrid also asserted that the house was formerly used as a public house, an inn, when meetings took place here. The curator, Miss Neidlinger, later confirmed this. Also, Ingrid felt that among the families living in the area, most of the members served in the patriot militia, but that there were occasional traitors, such as George Taylor. Colonel George Taylor might have been the man to whom Ingrid was referring. As for the man who was hanged, it would have been Captain Huddy, and he was hanged for having caused the death of a certain Philip White. Captain Joshua Huddy had been unjustly accused of having caused the death of the patriot Philip White and despite his innocence, was lynched by the patriots. Again, Ingrid had touched on something very real from history.

But the ghostly lady and the man who was hanged and the man who stared out the window onto the bay are not the only ghosts at the spy house. On the Fourth of July, 1975, a group of local boys were in the house in the blue and white room upstairs. Suddenly, the sewing machine door opened by itself and the pedals worked themselves without benefit of human feet. One of the boys looked up, and in the mirror in the bureau across, he could see a face with a long beard.

Another boy looked down the hall and there he saw a figure with a tall black hat and a long beard and sort of very full trousers as they were worn in an earlier age. That was enough for them and they ran from the house and never went back again.

One of the ladies who assists the curator, Agnes Lyons, refuses to do any typing in the upstairs room because the papers simply will not stand still. A draft seems to go by all the time and blow the papers to the floor even though the windows are closed. A Mrs. Lillian Boyer also saw the man with the beard standing at the top of the stairs, wearing a black hat and dressed in the period of the later 1700s. He had very large eyes, and seemed to be a man in his forties. He just stood there looking at her and she of course wouldn't pass him. Then he seemed to flash some sort of light back and forth, a brilliant light like a flashlight. And there were footsteps all over the house at the same time. She could even hear the man breathe, yet he was a ghost!

If you want to visit the spy house, address yourself to Gertrude Neidlinger, Curator, at the Spy House, postal address, Port Monmouth, New Jersey 07758. She's a gracious lady and I'm sure will make you welcome.

8

The Ghost Servants of Ringwood Manor
New Jersey

One of the most interesting haunted houses I ever visited is only an hour's drive from New York City, in northern New Jersey, not far from Saddle River. It is a manor house known locally as Ringwood Manor and it is considered one

of the more important historical houses in New Jersey. Built on land purchased by the Ogden family in 1740, it originally was the home of the owners of a successful iron smelting furnace. The area had many iron smelting furnaces during the late Colonial period when this kind of business was still profitable.

The main portion of the house dates back to 1762. Eventually, it became the property of Robert Erskine, the geographer of George Washington. The local iron business soared to great heights as a result of the revolutionary War, and the profits enabled Martin Ryerson, the later owner of Ringwood Manor, to rebuild it completely in 1807, tearing down the original old house.

However, after the iron business fell off in the 1830s, the house was sold to Peter Cooper and eventually passed to his son-in-law Abram S. Hewitt, one-time mayor of New York, Mrs. Hewitt changed the rather drab house into a mansion of 51 rooms, very much in the style of the early Victorian era. She moved various smaller buildings, already existing on the grounds, next to the main house, thereby giving it a somewhat offbeat appearance. In 1936, Erskine Hewitt left the estate to the State of New Jersey, and the mansion is now a museum which can be visited daily for a small fee. Not too many visitors come, however, since Ringwood Manor does not get the kind of attention some of the better-publicized national shrines attract.

I visited Ringwood Manor in the company of Ethel Johnson Meyers to follow up on persistent reports of hauntings in the old mansion. One of the chief witnesses to the ghostly goings-on was the superintendent of the manor, Alexander Waldron. He had heard footsteps when there was no one about, footsteps of two different people, indicating two entities. Doors that had been shut at night were found standing wide open in the morning when no one human could have done it. The feeling of "presences" in various parts of the house persisted. There is a local tradition that the ghost of Robert Erskine walks about with a lantern, but there is no evidence to substantiate this legend.

As a result of my investigation and Mrs. Meyers' trance, I discovered that the restless one—at least, one of them—was a so-called "Jackson White," living at the house at one time. The Jackson Whites are said to be a mixture of Negro and Indian and White races. They are descendants of runaway slaves who settled in parts of New Jersey in the nineteenth century and lived among the hill folk.

The center of the hauntings seems to be what was once the area of Mrs. Erskine's bedroom, but all along the corridors both upstairs and downstairs there are spots where a sensitive person might experience chills or cold clammy feelings. I made contact with the surviving personality of Mrs. Erskine, as well as an unhappy servant whose name was Jeremiah.

Jeremiah complained bitterly about his mistress who had mistreated him, he claimed. The ghost lady whose manor we were visiting, was not too pleased with our presence. Through the mouth of the medium in trance, she told us several times to get off her property! She may still be there, for all I know.

9

The Conference House Ghosts
New York City

Peace conferences may go on for years and years without yielding tangible results—so it is a refreshing thought to remember that a peace conference held on Staten Island between Lord Howe, the British commander in America, and a Congressional committee consisting of Benjamin Franklin, John Adams, and Edward Rutledge lasted but a single day—September 11, 1976, to be exact.

The position was this: the British were already in command of New York, Long Island and Staten Island, and the Yankees still held New Jersey and Pennsylvania, with Philadelphia as the seat of the Continental Congress. In view of his tremendous successes in the war against the colonists, Lord Howe felt that the suppression of the independence movement was only a matter of weeks. Wanting to avoid further bloodshed and, incidentally, to save himself some trouble, he suggested that a peace conference he held to determine whether an honorable peace could be concluded at that juncture of events.

Congress received his message with mixed emotions, having but lately worked out internal differences of opinion concerning the signing of the Declaration of Independence. A committee was appointed, consisting of the aforementioned three men, and empowered to investigate the offer. The three legislators went by horse to Perth Amboy, New Jersey, and were met at the New Jersey shore by a barge manned by British soldiers under a safe-conduct pass across the bay. They landed on the Staten Island shore and walked up to Bentley Manor, the residence of Lord Howe. There they were met with politeness and courtesies but also with a display of British might, for there were soldiers in full battle dress lined up along the road.

Later, the flamboyant John Adams told of soldiers "looking as fierce as ten furies, and making all the grimaces and gestures and motions of their muskets, with bayonets fixed, which, I suppose, military etiquette requires, but which we neither understood nor regarded."

Lord Howe outlined his plan for a settlement, explaining that it was futile for the Americans to carry on the war and that the British were willing to offer peace with honor. Of course, any settlement would involve the colonies' remaining under British rule. The three envoys listened in polite silence, after which Benjamin Franklin informed Lord Howe that the Declaration of Independence had already been signed on July 4, 1776, and that they would never go back under British rule.

The conference broke up, and Lord Howe, still very polite, had the trio conveyed to Amboy in his own barge, under the safe-conduct pass he had granted them. The following day, September 12, 1776, the War of Independence entered a new round: the Yankees knew what the British government was willing to offer them in order to obtain peace, and they realized that they might very well win the war with just a little more effort. Far from discouraging them, the failure of the peace conference on Staten Island helped reinforce the Continental Congress in its determination to pursue the War of Independence to its very end.

This historical event took place in a manor house overlooking Raritan Bay, and at the time, and for many years afterward, it was considered the most outstanding building on Staten Island. The two-story white building goes back to before 1680 and is a colonial manor built along British lines. It was erected by a certain Christopher Billopp, a somewhat violent and hardheaded sea captain who had served in the British Navy for many years. Apparently, Captain Billopp had friends at court in London, and when the newly appointed Governor Andros came to America in 1674, he gave

Billopp a patent as lieutenant of a company of soldiers. In the process, Billopp acquired nearly one thousand acres of choice land on Staten Island. But Billopp got into difficulties with his governor and re-entered navy service for awhile, returning to Staten Island under Governor Thomas Dongan. In 1687 he received a land grant for Bentley Manor, sixteen hundred acres of very choice land, and on this tract he built the present manor house. The Billopp family were fierce Tories and stood with the Crown to the last. The Captain's grandson, also named Christopher, who was already born in the manor, lived there till the end of the Revolution, when he moved to New Brunswick, Canada, along with many other Tories who could not stay on in the newly independent colonies.

From then on, the manor house had a mixed history of owners and gradually fell into disrepair. Had it not been built so solidly, with the keen eye of a navy man's perception of carpentry, perhaps none of it would stand today. As it was, an association was formed in 1920 to restore the historical landmark to its former glory. This has now been done, and the Conference House, as it is commonly called, is a museum open to the public. It is located in what was once Bentley Manor but today is called Tottenville, and it can easily be reached from New York City via the Staten Island Ferry. The ground floor contains two large rooms and a staircase leading to the upper story, which is also divided into two rooms. In the basement is a kitchen and a vault-like enclosure. Both basement and attic are of immense proportions. The large room downstairs to the left of the entrance was originally used as a dining room and the room to the right as a parlor. Upstairs, the large room to the left is a bedroom while the one to the right is nowadays used as a Benjamin Franklin museum. In between the two large rooms is a small room, perhaps a child's room at one time. At one time there also was a tunnel from the vault in the basement to the water's edge, which was used as a means of escape during Indian attacks, a frequent occurrence in early Colonial days. Also, this secret tunnel could be used to obtain supplies by the sea route without being seen by observers on land.

As early as 1962 I was aware of the Conference House and its reputation of being haunted. My initial investigation turned up a lot of hearsay evidence, hardly of a scientific nature, but nevertheless of some historial significance inasmuch as there is usually a grain of truth in all legendary stories. According to the local legends, Captain Billopp had jilted his fiancée, and she had died of a broken heart in the house. As a result, strange noises, including murmurs, sighs, moans, and pleas of an unseen voice, were reported to have been heard in the house as far back as the mid-nineteenth century. According to the old Staten Island newspaper *The Transcript*, the phenomena were heard by a number of workmen during the restoration of the house after it had been taken over as a museum.

My first visit to the Conference House took place in 1962, in the company of Ethel Johnson Meyers and two of her friends, Rose de Simone and Pearl Winder, who had come along for the ride since they were interested in the work Mrs. Meyers and I were doing. Mrs. Meyers, of course, had no idea where we were going or why we were visiting Staten Island. Nevertheless, when we were still about a half-hour's ride away from the house, she volunteered her impressions of the place we were going to. When I encouraged her to speak freely, she said that the house she had yet to see was white, that the ground floor was divided into two rooms, and that the east room contained a brown table and eight chairs. She also stated that the room to the west of the entrance was the larger room of the two, and that some silverware was on display in that room.

When we arrived at the house, I checked these statements at once; they were entirely correct, except that the number of chairs was seven, not eight as Mrs. Meyers had stated. I questioned the resident curator about this seeming discrepancy. One of the chairs and the silverware had indeed been on display for years but had been removed from the room eight years prior to our visit.

"Butler," Mrs. Meyers mumbled as we entered the house. It turned out that the estate next to Bentley belonged to the Butlers; undoubtedly, members of that family had been in the Conference House many times. As is my custom, I allowed my medium free rein of her intuition. Mrs. Meyers decided to settle on the second-story room to the left of the staircase, where she sat down on the floor for want of a chair.

Gradually entering the vibrations of the place, she spoke of a woman named Jane whom she described as being stout, white-haired, and dressed in a dark green dress and a fringed shawl. Then the medium looked up at me and, as if she intuitively knew the importance of her statement, simply said, "Howe." This shook me up, since Mrs. Meyers had no knowledge of Lord Howe's connection with the place she was in. I also found interesting Mrs. Meyer's description of a "presence," that is to say, a ghost, whom she described as a big man in a fur hat, being rather fat and wearing a skin coat and high boots, a brass-buckled belt, and black trousers. "I feel boats around him, nets, sailing boats, and I feel a broad foreign accent," Mrs. Meyers stated, adding that she saw him in a four-masted ship of a square-rigger type. At the same time she mentioned the initial T. What better description of the Tory, Captain Billopp, could she have given!

"I feel as if I am being dragged somewhere by Indians," Mrs. Meyers suddenly exclaimed, as I reported in my original account of this case in my first book *Ghost Hunter*. "There is violence, and somebody dies on a pyre of wood. Two men, one white, one Indian; and on two sticks nearby are their scalps." It seemed to me that what Mrs. Meyers had tuned in on were remnants of emotional turmoil in the early colonial days; as I have noted, Indian attacks were quite frequent during the early and middle parts of the eighteenth century.

When we went down into the cellar, Mrs. Meyers assured us that six people had been buried near the front wall during the Revolutionary War and that they were all British soldiers. She also said that eight more were buried somewhere else on the grounds, and she had the impression that the basement had been used as a hospital during an engagement. Later investigation confirmed that members of the Billopp family had been buried on the grounds near the road and that British soldiers might very well have been buried there too, since there were frequent skirmishes around the house from July, 1776, to the end of the year. Captain Billopp was twice kidnapped from his own house by armed bands operating from the New Jersey Shore.

It was clear to me that Mrs. Meyers was entering various layers of history and giving us bits and pieces of her impressions, not necessarily in the right order but as she received them. The difficulty with trance mediumship is that you cannot direct it the way you want to, that is to say, ferret out just those entities or layers from the past you are interested in. You have to take "pot luck," as it were, hoping that sufficient material of interest will come through the medium.

Once more we returned to the upper part of the house. Suddenly, Mrs. Meyers turned white in the face and held on for dear life to the winding staircase. For a moment she seemed immobilized. Then, coming to life again, she slowly descended the stairs and pointed to a spot near the landing of the second story. "A woman was killed here with a crooked knife!" she said.

Aha, I thought, there is our legend about Captain Billopp and his jilted fiancée. But he didn't kill her; she had died of a broken heart. Mrs. Earley, the custodian, was trying to be helpful, so I questioned her about any murder that might have occurred in the house. "Why, yes," she obliged. "Captain Billopp once flew into a rage and killed a female slave on that very spot on the stairs." As she spoke, I had the impression that the custodian was shuddering just a little herself.

From time to time people had told me of their visits to the Conference House and wondered whether the "ghost in residence" was still active. Finally, I asked a young lady I had been working with for some time to try her hand at picking up whatever might be left in the atmosphere of the Conference House. Ingrid Beckman, an artist by profession, knew very little about the house but had access to the short account of my investigation given in *Ghost Hunter*.

I asked Ingrid to go to the house by herself, and on the afternoon of November 25, 1972, she paid a visit.

In order to avoid tourists, she had arrived at the house about one o'clock. The house was still closed to visitors so she sat down on a bench outside. "I walked around, and even on the outside I felt a presence," Ingrid began her report to me. "I felt as if the place were really alive. Then I went up to the front porch and peeked into the main hallway, and when I looked up the stairs I had a feeling of gloom and foreboding. I had the distinct sensation of a dangerous situation there."

Strangely enough, Ingrid seemed to have been led to that house. Two weeks prior to her visit, she had happened to find herself in Nyack, New York, browsing through some antique shops. There she met a woman who started to talk to her. The woman explained that she was from Staten Island, and when she discovered that Ingrid lived there also, she suggested that Ingrid visit a certain house, once the property of an old sea captain. The house, the lady said, had an interesting tunnel which began behind a fireplace and ran down to the water's edge. Ingrid, always interested in visiting old houses, had promised to look into the matter. This was two weeks before I mentioned a visit to the Conference House to her.

The following weekend, Ingrid was with some friends at her apartment on Staten Island. She took the opportunity of asking whether any of them had ever heard of the house as described by her acquaintance. One of the young men present affirmed that there was such a house, called the Conference House, and that it was haunted by the spirit of a slave who had been killed there. That was on Sunday. The following Monday I telephoned Ingrid with the request to go to the Conference House.

As Ingrid was sitting on the front porch of the house, waiting for the door to be opened, she had the distinct feeling that someone was watching her. "I felt as if someone knew I was there," she explained, "and I especially felt this coming from the window about the hallway. It is a crooked window, and I felt that it had some sort of significance. If anyone were looking at me or wanted to get my attention, it would be through that window. But when I went in, as soon as the door had been opened to visitors, the first place I went to was the basement. As I was looking around the basement, I came upon a little archway, as if I had been *directed* to go there."

The spot made her literally jump; she felt that something terrible had occurred near the fireplace, and she experienced heavy chills at the same time; someone had been brutalized at the entrance to the tunnel. Fortunately, she had managed to go there by herself, having discouraged the tourist guide from taking her around. "The tunnel entrance is particularly terrorizing," Ingrid said. "This tunnel caused me chills all the way up to my neck."

Finally tearing herself away from the basement, she went up the stairs, again by herself. Immediately she arrived at the upper landing and went to the bedroom to the left; as she stood in the entranceway, she heard a noise like a knock.

"The hallway upstairs felt terrible," Ingrid explained. "I turned around and looked down the stairs. As I looked, I almost became dizzy. It felt as if someone had been pushed down them or hurt on them." To be sure that she wasn't imagining things or being influenced by what she had read, Ingrid decided to go up and down those stairs several times. Each time, the sensation was the same. On one of her trips up the stairs, she ascertained that the window, which had so attracted her while she was still waiting outside, was indeed just outside the haunted stairwell.

"I got the impression of a slave woman, especially in the upstairs bedroom; I also felt there was a disturbance around the table downstairs, but I don't think the two are connected. I felt the woman was associated with the upstairs bedroom and the stairway and possibly the tunnel entrance; but the feeling in the basement is another episode, I think."

"What period do you think the disturbances go back to?" I asked.

"I'd say the 1700s, going back before the Revolution."

"Do you have the feeling that there is still something there that hasn't been fully resolved?"

"Yes, definitely. I think that is why I had such strong vibrations about it, and I think that is also why I got the information two weeks beforehand."

"Do you think that it is a man or a woman who is 'hung up' in there?"

"I think it is a woman, but there may also be a man because the scene at the table had something to do with a man. He may have been shot, or he may have been abducted from that room—you know, taken through the tunnel."

I suddenly recalled that Captain Billopp was twice abducted by Yankee irregulars from the Jersey shore. Gabriel Disosway, in his 1946 account of the Manor of Bentley, reported that "Colonel Billopp, at the time a warm party man and military leader, was closely watched, and, it is said, was twice taken from his own house by armed bands from 'the Jerseys,' and thus made a prisoner. Amboy is in sight, and upon one of these occasions, he was observed by some Americans, who had stationed themselves with a spy glass in the church steeple of that town. As soon as they saw him enter his abode, they ran to their boats, rapidly crossed the river, and he was soon their captive."

On January 28, 1973, Ingrid made another, spontaneous visit to the Conference House. She had much the same impressions as before, but this time she managed to speak to the caretaker. The lady admitted hearing heavy footsteps upstairs at times, which sounded to her like those of a man wearing heavy boots with spurs attached. Also, on the anniversary of the "the murder," the caretaker claims to have seen a man run up the stairs toward a girl waiting on the first landing. "Her story is that the girl was beheaded," Ingrid reported further. "She says that one afternoon last summer, as she was dusting the room on the left of the ground floor, she could put her hand 'right through' a British soldier! This past summer her daughter from South Carolina came to visit and insisted on staying upstairs in the haunted rooms. That night the daughter allegedly heard a man's laughter, followed by a woman's laughter, and then a shriek. According to the caretaker, this happens at regular intervals."

10

Aaron Burr's Haunted Stables
New York City

Aaron Burr, one-time vice-president of the United States, was a colorful political figure who is perhaps best remembered for the duel he fought with Alexander Hamilton at Weehawken, New Jersey, in which Hamilton was killed. Even though the duel was a fair fight, and in terms of the early nineteenth century a legitimate undertaking, Burr was accused of having murdered the brilliant young Hamilton and had to flee for his life. Burr's political career was affected and in the end the Hamilton death prevented him from rising higher, perhaps becoming president of the United States.

This embittered him, and at a later date he led an expedition to the West to open up new territories. His political enemies accused him of sedition, of trying to start a new state in the West, and he was brought to trial. However, he was found not guilty of sedition. Nevertheless, this contributed to his further downfall and Aaron Burr died an embittered, unhappy man. The untimely death of his daughter Theodosia, aboard a ship lost at sea, also helped break him down early in life.

Down in Greenwich Village, New York's artistic district, on West 3rd Street at the corner of Sullivan Street there is a café which was known as the Café Bizarre, until sometime ago; it now houses a restaurant. This is a very well-preserved, three-story building dating back to pre-Revolutionary times and remodeled in the early nineteenth century. It is probably one of the oldest buildings in the area. At one time it formed part of Aaron Burr's stables, and prior to Burr's ownership, belonged to a British colonial family. The records show that Aaron Burr used it well into the 1830s, but beyond that time and beyond Burr's death, the usage the building was put to is not clear.

The ground floor portion of the building is a kind of duplex loft, properly decorated for a night club with a bizarre motif. The rear section of this room has been the center of ghostly manifestations. I have investigated the place on two occasions. A ghostly apparition of what may very well have been Aaron Burr, from the description, has appeared to a number of people working at the Café Bizarre. A waiter and the owner's wife, Mrs. Renee Allman, have described the intense-looking man in a white ruffled shirt with piercing black eyes and short beard.

A visitor to the Café Bizarre, a young girl by the name of Alice McDermott, also had a psychic experience in which she saw the same figure. As a result of my two investigations with mediums Ethel Johnson and later Sybil Leek, Mr. Burr's restless personality was freed from the place where so many emotional memories had kept him captive.

The trance interrogation was particularly dramatic. At first, the entity speaking through Mrs. Leek evaded my questions concerning its identity. At no time did "he" admit to being the late Aaron Burr. That was hardly necessary. Under questioning, the spirit spoke of conditions only Burr would have been familiar with in these surroundings. For instance, at the very outset, the spirit cried out for Theo, asking me to find her for him. Theo had been Burr's only daughter, whom he had lost early in life. She was aboard a ship that never reached her destination and to this day we don't know whether the ship sank in a storm or fell victim to piracy.

Theodosia is a very unusual name. Only the Burr family used it for its women during the period under investigation.

Another reason why I found the identity of the spirit convincing involved Burr's exile in France. Under questioning (and without prodding or leading questions on my part), the entity spoke of spending time in France. He spoke of wearing a beard and having to hide from his enemies. When I insisted that he tell me his name, he mentioned the name Arnot. Later research disclosed that Burr did have to hide from Napoleon's police, that he had a short beard when he returned from his French exile, and that the cover name he had used while in France was indeed Arnot. None of this could have been know to Mrs. Leek, or, for that matter, to me.

If you want to visit the place, remember that it is no long the Café Bizarre but a different restaurant. The present owners may have no idea as to the background or history of the place. But you may still pick up the vibrations from the past though I doubt very much that Burr is still about.

11

The Old Merchant's House Ghosts
New York City

You may remember an old movie called "The Heiress," in which Olivia de Haviland fought against the iron will of her stern father who did not want her to marry a fortune hunter. Consequently, the heiress, as the girl was called, shut herself off from the world, having been denied the man she loved, and died a recluse in her old mansion.

The film itself was based on the well known novel, "Washington Square," by Henry James. James lived in the area and knew its history well indeed. The James novel is certainly based on fact, although he has embellished it with the freedom generally afforded novelists. The house, you see, didn't stand on Washington Square, in New York City, but was not too far away from it. It is called the "Old Merchant's House," and currently is accessible to visitors as a local museum maintained privately but open to the public at certain hours.

Surrounded by old houses, some of which are in a sad state of disrepair, the Old Merchant's House at 29 East Fourth Street, Manhattan, stands out like a jewel in a generally low-class neighborhood, not far from the Bowery where derelicts are still seen to this day, homeless men and women who make their precarious living by begging.

The house became the property of Seabury Tredwell, a wealthy merchant in the hardware business, as soon as it was completed by its builder. It is a Federal-style building with windows opening onto Fourth Street. Originally, a lovely garden surrounded the house, but today the garden is gone. The entrance is particularly imposing, with two col-

umns in classical style at the top of a few steps, and wrought-
iron lanterns adorning the door. There are three floors top-
ped by an attic, and there is also a basement.

Inside, the furniture is still of that period. There is a
banister by Duncan Phyfe, and a fine staircase leading to the
upper three stories. The downstairs is filled with fine furniture, some of it also by Duncan Phyfe, a rectangular piano
which is still there, and in showcases along the walls one
finds some of the costumes left behind.

The ghostly phenomena in the house center around
Tredwell's three daughters, Phoebe, Sarah and Gertrude.
According to tradition, Mr. Tredwell did not take kindly to
any suitor who seemed to want to marry his daughters for
their financial status.

The main manifestations occurred in the kitchen on
the ground floor level in the rear of the house. But what used
to be Gertrude's bedroom upstairs also has a presence in it
from time to time. The ghost is that of a small elegant woman
dressed in the finery of the middle nineteenth century. That
this is Gertrude herself is very likely, since, according to my
psychic friend Ethel Johnson Meyers, it was she who died
tragically here. There had been an unwanted baby, followed
by disapproval of her actions by her family. How much of this
can be proven objectively is doubtful, but a presence has
been observed in the Old Merchant's House by several reliable witnesses, and no attempt has been made to exorcise
her, since, after all, this was her home.

One need not dwell upon the ghostly manifestations,
as far as the curator is concerned, because she may not be
aware of them. But I suggest a visit to the kitchen area, the
back bedroom upstairs, and Gertrude's front bedroom. It
contains a small canopied bed, which, according to at least
one witness, is haunted.

One eerie story told about the Old Merchant's House
concerns the fireplace on the third floor. Allegedly, it cannot
be photographed. I tried my luck with a very good camera
while a professional photographer who was with me at the
time also photographed the fireplace. Although the fireplace

did appear on both pictures, there is a strange white area around it that cannot be accounted for.

The Old Merchant's House merits a visit if only as an historical landmark and because of the well-preserved costumes and utensils of a bygone era. There is a fascinating trapdoor on one of the upper floors, connected perhaps with the secret rendezvous between Gertrude and her gentleman friend outside the house. At the time the house had a garden, and the river was not too far away. It was possible to approach the house on the East River, walk up the slanting acreage, which was then largely open, and visit the house. On the other hand, research has indicated that secret passageways existed between many of the houses in the area and the river, perhaps remnants of the Revolutionary period when escape from dangers made such precautions advisable.

Gertrude's own clothes are still preserved in the showcases and nothing in the house has been changed from its original appearance. When the house was restored by a private committee of concerned citizens, great pains were taken to present everything the way it was when the house was at its best. Architect Joseph Roberto was in charge of these sensitive restorations, and it is largely to his credit that the Old Merchant's House today presents a truly major historical attraction, as well as the tantalizing prospect of meeting up with the dainty ghost of Gertrude Tredwell herself coming down the stairs to greet the visitor.

12

The Ghosts at the Jumel-Morris Mansion
New York City

You wouldn't think that in the bustling city of New York, right in the heart of Manhattan there stands a magnificent southern-styled mansion with several ghosts in it. But the fact of the matter is there is such a building, nowadays known as the Morris-Jumel mansion in Washington Heights, Manhattan, at the corner of 160th Street and Edgecombe Avenue. I've been to this mansion several times, twice as part of an investigation into the hauntings reported and several times more with friends, some of whom felt chilly and disturbed by the continuing presences in the building.

Built at the highest spot of Manhattan originally called Harlem Heights, the mansion was erected by the British-born Colonel Roger Morris and in 1776, during the Revolutionary War, General George Washington made it his headquarters during the battle of Long Island. Later on, when the fortunes of war changed, the British moved in again, and General Sir Henry Clinton stayed at the mansion. From then on, the career of this magnificent building was somewhat checkered. At one point it served as an ordinary tavern called Calumet Hall.

One day in 1810 a French wine merchant, by the name of Stephen Jumel, recently arrived on these shores, and his ambitious American-born wife passed by and decided to buy the place on the spot. At that time the property included 35 acres of land surrounding it. Madame Jumel immediately refurbished and renovated the place and it soon became one of the show places of New York City.

There are four stories and a basement and the principal areas of psychic activity are the second and third floors as well as the balcony which can be seen from a distance away. It was on that balcony on January 19, 1964, that a small group of school children saw the ghost of Madame Jumel. It all happened when they were waiting to be let into the historical building.

They had arrived a little early, and were becoming restless, when one of the children pointed to the balcony where a lady in a flimsy violet-colored gown had just appeared. "Shush!" she said to the children, trying to calm them down. After that, she simply receded into the room behind the balcony. It never occurred to the children until later that she had never opened the doors but had simply vanished through *the closed doors.* When the curator at that time, Mrs. Emma Bingay Campbell, arrived to let them in, they complained that they could have been in the house much sooner and why didn't the lady on the balcony open up for them? Needless to say there was no lady on the balcony as far as the curator was concerned. But she soon realized that she was presiding over a much-haunted house.

One flight up in what used to be Madame Jumel's own bedroom I held a seance with the help of Ethel Johnson Meyers, during which the late Stephen Jumel complained bitterly about being murdered by his own wife. He had fallen off a haywagon and hurt himself on a pitchfork, and a doctor had been summoned to attend to his wounds. As soon as the doctor had left, however, Mrs. Jumel tore off the bandages and Stephen bled to death. I tried to have his tomb in a nearby cemetery opened but never received official permission to do so.

The one-time Vice President of the United States, Aaron Burr, a famous political figure of the first half of the nineteenth century, was even then friendly with the later Widow Jumel. He, in fact, married her and spent much time at the mansion. His presence has also been felt by many visitors.

As if having an angry victim of foul play in the house and perhaps the lingering spirit of Madame Jumel herself were not enough, there is also a young servant girl who became involved with one of the family and committed suicide by jumping out the window. She may be one of the ghosts, having been observed on the top floor where the servants' quarters were located. Since I conducted two "rescue" seances at the mansion during which Stephen Jumel

had the opportunity to complain about his untimely death, I feel that he has been pacified and is no longer a resident of the Morris-Jumel mansion. But Madame Jumel herself and the servant girl may well still roam the corridors of the house where they once lived, the one in unusual splendor, the other in great anguish.

Not long ago a school teacher brought his class from a nearby school to visit the famed mansion. While the children were inspecting the lower two floors he dashed up to the top floor, being a history buff most eager to inspect the house from top to bottom. Picture his surprise when he was confronted by a Revolutionary soldier who had practically stepped out of a painting on the top floor! The teacher fainted on the spot and was revived later.

Not so lucky was another visitor, again a teacher, who, having a history of heart disease, was frightened to death on one of the floors. But this is unusual: ghosts do not hurt people, ghosts should not frighten people because they are, after all, only human beings in trouble *with themselves*.

The Morris-Jumel mansion can be visited every day until 4:00 P.M. It is maintained as a museum and there is no special reservation necessary to visit. However, certain rooms of the upper floors have been closed off to the public now, whether for reasons of expediency or because of the continuing strong interests in ghosts is hard to say. The personnel serving in the mansion know nothing about the ghostly manifestations, so there is no point in questioning them about it.

13

The Ghosts at
St. Mark's in-The-Bouwerie
New York City

There really isn't any reason why churches should not
also be haunted at times, but somehow the idea of holy
ground harboring restless souls does not occur to the average
person. Nevertheless, there are a respectable number of such
edifices around the world. One of the most colorful ones is

the church of St. Mark's in downtown New York City, standing at the corner of Second Avenue and Tenth Street. This area has lately become hippie land, but is reasonably safe in the daytime.

The church itself was built in 1799 on the site of an earlier chapel going back to Peter Stuyvesant and the year 1660. The governor himself is buried in the crypt, which can be seen. The last member of the Stuyvesant family died in 1953, and the crypt was sealed.

Built along the neoclassical lines, the church stands in lonely majesty in a garden plot which serves in part as a cemetery. This is surrounded by a cast iron fence, and it seems like an oasis amid the somber-looking utilitarian apartment houses and shops. The church is open in the daytime and one need not obtain permission from anyone to visit it. Although not all rectors feel the same way about ghostly apparitions at their church, my witnesses were all respectable, sane people.

There were two or possibly three ghosts at St. Mark's, and for all I know, they are still there since no attempt to exorcise them has been made. One is a woman parishioner who appears in the middle of the nave in the central aisle. Another entity has, on occasion, shown up on the balcony close to the magnificent organ. The ghostly woman has also been observed closer to the entrance door in the rear of the building. Finally, there are the sounds of a man walking with a cane, and it has been thought that this indicates Peter Stuyvesant himself—Father Knickerbocker of the legend—who had a wooden leg and did indeed walk with a cane. It is possible that his death might not have been entirely final for this restless soul. The woman ghost, however, is still in evidence and has been observed as recently as two or three years ago. A short time ago a fire nearly destroyed the old church, allegedly caused by the cigarette of a careless worker. With the help of many neighborhood volunteers the church has since been fully restored, though not quite as it was: still, to the ghostly parishioners it must be a welcome sight to be back in the familiar surroundings!

14

A Ghost in Greenwich Village
New York City

Up to 1956, the ancient studio building at 51 West 10th Street was a landmark known to many connoisseurs of old New York, but it was demolished to make way for one of those nondescript, modern apartment buildings that are gradually taking away the charm of Greenwich Village, and give us doubtful comforts in its stead.

Until the very last, reports of an apparition, allegedly the ghost of artist John La Farge, who died in 1910, continued to come in. A few houses down the street is the Church of the Ascension; the altar painting, "The Ascension," is the work of John La Farge. Actually, the artist did the work on the huge painting at his studio, Number 22, in 51 West 10th Street. He finished it, however, in the church itself, "in place." Having just returned from the Orient, La Farge used a new technique involving the use of several coats of paint, thus making the painting heavier than expected. The painting was hung, but the chassis collapsed; La Farge built a stronger chassis and the painting stayed in place this time. Years went by. Oliver La Farge, the noted novelist and grandson of the painter, had spent much of his youth with his celebrated grandfather. One day, while working across the street, he was told the painting had fallen again. Dashing across the street, he found that the painting had indeed fallen, and that his grandfather had died *that very instant!*

The fall of the heavy painting was no trifling matter to La Farge, who was equally as well known as an architect as he was a painter. Many buildings in New York for which he drew the plans 75 years ago are still standing. But the construction of the chassis of the altar painting may have been faulty. And therein lies the cause for La Farge's ghostly visitations, it would seem. The artists at No. 51 insisted always that La Farge could not find rest until he had corrected his calculations, searching for the original plans of the chassis to find out what was wrong. An obsession to redeem himself as an artist and craftsman, then, would be the underlying cause for the persistence with which La Farge's ghost returned to his old haunts.

The first such return was reported in 1944, when a painter by the name of Feodor Rimsky and his wife lived in No. 22. Late one evening, they returned from the opera. On approaching their studio, they noticed that a light was on and the door open, although they distinctly remembered having *left it shut*. Rimsky walked into the studio, pushed aside the heavy draperies at the entrance to the studio itself, and stopped in amazement. In the middle of the room, a single lamp plainly revealed a stranger behind the large chair in what Rimsky called his library corner; the man wore a tall black hat and a dark, billowing velvet coat. Rimsky quickly told his wife to wait, and rushed across the room to get a closer look at the intruder. But the man *just vanished* as the painter reached the chair.

Later, Rimsky told of his experience to a former owner of the building, who happened to be an amateur historian. He showed Rimsky some pictures of former tenants of his building. In two of them, Rimsky easily recognized his visitor, wearing exactly the same clothes Rimsky had seen him in. Having come from Europe but recently, Rimsky knew nothing of La Farge and had never seen a picture of him. The ball dress worn by the ghost had not been common at the turn of the century, but La Farge was known to affect such strange attire.

Three years later, the Rimskys were entertaining some guests at their studio, including an advertising man named William Weber, who was known to have had psychic experiences in the past. But Weber never wanted to discuss this "special talent" of his, for fear of being ridiculed. As the conversation flowed among Weber, Mrs. Weber, and two other guests, the advertising man's wife noticed her husband's sudden stare at a cabinet on the other side of the room, where paintings were stored. She saw nothing, but Weber asked her in an excited tone of voice—"Do you see that man in the cloak and top hat over there?"

Weber knew nothing of the ghostly tradition of the studio or of John La Farge; no stranger could have gotten by the door without being noticed, and no one had been expected at this hour. The studio was locked from the *inside*.

After that, the ghost of John La Farge was heard many times by a variety of tenants at No. 51, opening windows or pushing draperies aside, but not until 1948 was he *seen* again.

Up a flight of stairs from Studio 22, but connected to it—artists like to visit each other—was the studio of illustrator John Alan Maxwell. Connecting stairs and a "secret rest room" used by La Farge had long been walled up in the many structural changes in the old building. Only the window of the walled-up room was still visible from the outside. It was in this area that Rimsky felt that the restless spirit of John La Farge was trapped. As Miss Archer puts it in her narrative, "walled in like the Golem, sleeping through the day and close to the premises for roaming through the night."

After many an unsuccessful search of Rimsky's studio, apparently the ghost started to look in Maxwell's studio. In the spring of 1948, the ghost of La Farge made his initial appearance in the illustrator's studio.

It was a warm night, and Maxwell had gone to bed naked, pulling the covers over himself. Suddenly he awakened. From the amount of light coming in through the skylight, he judged the time to be about one or two in the morning. *He had the uncanny feeling of not being alone in the room.* As his eyes got used to the darkness, he clearly distinguished the figure of a tall woman, bending over his bed, lifting and straightening his sheets several times over. Behind her, there was a man staring at a wooden filing cabinet at the foot of the couch. Then he opened a drawer, looked in it, and closed it again. Getting hold of himself, Maxwell noticed that the woman wore a light red dress of the kind worn in the last century, and the man a white shirt and dark cravat of the same period. It never occurred to the illustrator that they were anything but *people*; probably, he thought, models in costume working for one of the artists in the building.

The woman then turned to her companion as if to say something, but did not, and walked off toward the dark room at the other end of the studio. The man then went back to the cabinet and leaned on it, head in hand. By now Maxwell had regained his wits and thought the intruders must be burglars, although he could not figure out how they had entered his place, since he had locked it from the *inside* before going to bed! Making a fist, he struck at the stranger, yelling, "Put your hands up!"

His voice could be heard clearly along the empty corridors. *But his fist went through the man and into the filing cabinet.* Nursing his injured wrist, he realized that his visitors had dissolved into thin air. There was no one in the dark room. The door was still securely locked. The skylight, 150 feet above ground, could not very well have served as an escape route *to anyone human.* By now Maxwell knew that La Farge and his wife had paid him a social call.

Other visitors to No. 51 complained about strange winds and sudden chills when passing La Farge's walled-up room. One night, one of Maxwell's lady visitors returned, shortly after leaving his studio, in great agitation, yelling, "That man! That man!" The inner court of the building was glass-enclosed, so that one could see clearly across to the corridors of the other side of the building. Maxwell and his remaining guests saw nothing there.

But the woman insisted that she saw a strange man under one of the old gaslights in the building; he seemed to lean against the wall of the corridor, dressed in old-fashioned clothes and *possessed of a face so cadaverous and death-mask-like, that it set her a-screaming!*

This was the first time the face of the ghost had been observed clearly by anyone. The sight was enough to make her run back to Maxwell's studio. Nobody could have left without being seen through the glass-enclosed corridors and no one had seen a stranger in the building that evening. As usual, he had vanished into thin air.

Now there is a modern apartment building at 51 West 10th Street. Is John La Farge still roaming its ugly modern corridors? One night, I went into the Church of the Ascension, gazed at the marvelous altar painting, and prayed a little that he shouldn't *have to*.

15

The Haunting at the Poughkeepsie Rectory
New York State

A few years ago Bishop James Pike made news by publicly declaring that he had spoken with his dead son James in a séance arranged on Canadian television with the late medium Arthur Ford. Not much later he himself became news when he died near the Dead Sea, having run out of gas and water in the desert. A controversial figure both in life and afterlife, Bishop James Pike, onetime Bishop of California and the author of a number of remarkable books, was no stranger to psychic phenomena.

During my work with him, I got to know the Christ Church rectory in Poughkeepsie, New York, pretty well. In 1947 Pike had been offered the position of rector, and he spent two and one-half years there. Christ Church is a large, beautiful, almost modern Episcopal church. The altar, with its candles, indicates what are generally called "high church" attitudes, that is, closer to Roman Catholicism. The outside of the church has remained turn-of-the century, and so has the rectory attached immediately to the church itself. There is also a small library between rectory and church.

I asked permission of the rector of Christ Church to visit, and in July of 1968 I took medium Ethel Johnson Meyers there. She relived ̍practically the entire incident Bishop Pike had reported to me privately earlier.

What had occurred during James Pike's residency at Poughkeepsie was not unusual as hauntings go. To him it seemed merely puzzling, and he made no attempt to follow up on it in the way I did when I brought Mrs. Meyers to the scene. Pike had taken over his position at Poughkeepsie, replacing an elderly rector with diametrically opposed views in church matters. The former rector had died shortly afterward.

Pike soon found that his candles were being blown out, that doors shut of their own volition, and that objects overhead would move—or seemingly move—when in fact they did not. All the noises and disturbances did not particularly upset Bishop Pike. However, on one occasion he found himself faced with a bat, flying about madly in the library. Knowing that there was no way in or out of the library except by the door he had just opened, he immediately closed the door again and went to look for an instrument with which to capture the bat. When he returned and cautiously opened the door to the library, the bat had disappeared. There is no possible way by which the creature could have escaped.

16

The Ghost at West Point
New York State

So much history has taken place at the United States Military Academy at West Point, which used to be a fortress guarding the approaches of the Hudson River, it is not surprising that ghostly apparitions should have also occurred from time to time.

Four military cadets at the United States Military Academy saw the apparition of a soldier dressed in eighteenth century cavalry uniform, and according to the witnesses, the apparition seemed luminous and shimmering. Apparently, the ghost materialized out of the wall and a closet in room 4714 and on one occasion also from the middle of the floor. Once it ruffled the bathrobe of a cadet, and on another occasion it turned on a shower!

As soon as the publicity drew the attention of the guiding spirits (of the military kind) to the incident, room 4714 was emptied of its inhabitants. The room itself was then declared off-limits to one and all. Ghosts, of course, do not obey military authorities.

Cadet Captain Keith W. Bakken, however, was willing to discuss it. "There is no doubt about it at all," he said, "the room grew unnaturally cold." Two weeks before, he and another upperclassman spent a night sleeping in the room, their beds separated by a partition. At about 2:00 o'clock in the morning Cadet Bakken's companion began to shout. Bakken jumped from his bed and rounded the partition, but he could not see anything special. What he did feel, however, was an icy cold for which there was no rational explanation.

However, Bakken and his companion weren't the first ones to encounter the ghost. Two plebes who occupied room 4714 before them also saw it. The second time the apparition walked out of the bureau that stood in the middle of the floor. He heard the plebes shout, and ran into the room. One of the cadets who actually saw the apparition was able to furnish a drawing. It is the face of a man with a drooping moustache, a high old-fashioned cap surmounted by a feather. It is the uniform of a cavalry man of about two hundred years ago.

West Point has a number of ghostly legends; what is now the superintendent's mansion, allegedly has a 150-year-old ghostly girl, a woman named Molly, who in life was a camp follower.

Another cadet was taking a shower, prior to moving into the haunted room on the same floor and on leaving the shower noticed that his bathrobe was swinging back and forth on the hook. Since the door was closed and the window closed, there could be no breeze causing the robe to move. The building in which this occurred stands on old grounds;

an earlier barracks stood there, but had long since been demolished. Could it be that the ghostly cavalry man might have died there and been unable to adjust to his new surroundings?

If you visit West Point, and there are no restrictions to that, try to find the building that contains room 4714. Company G-4 is quartered there, and perhaps someone will help you find the way.

17

The Ghost at the Altar
Pennsylvania

Considering the fact that churches and religion in general should give us peace of mind, it may come as a surprise that even churches can be haunted by ghosts. But those who serve religion, priests, ministers and rabbis, are, after all, also human beings who may undergo emotional problems and stress. Such was the case in a large and beautiful church in Pennsylvania.

About an hour's drive from Pittsburgh, in the small town of Millvale, hard by the Allegheny River, stands an imposing stone church built at the turn of the last century. Positioned as it is on a bluff looking down toward the river, it seems somewhat out of place for so small a town as Millvale. Attached to the building are a school and rectory, and there is an air of clean efficiency about the entire complex.

This is a Roman Catholic church, and the priests are all of Yugoslav background. Thus, there is a peculiarity about the ritual, about the atmosphere inside the church, and about the men who serve here. The church is very large, and the altar is framed by original paintings in the Yugoslav style. They are the work of Maxim Hvatka, the celebrated Yugoslav artist who worked in the early part of this century and who died a few years ago. Near the altar there is a large eternal light—that is to say, an enclosed candle protected from drafts or other interference. This is important, since much of the phenomenon centers in this area and includes the blowing out of the eternal light by unknown causes.

Although the administrators of the church do not exactly cherish the notion that they have a ghost, there have

been a number of witnesses who have seen a figure pass by
the altar. The painter Hvatka himself saw the ghostly apparition while working on his frescoes. Chills, which could not
be accounted for, were also noted in the immediate area of
the eternal light.

There is nothing concerning the present-day church that would account for the apparition of a figure at the altar. However, prior to the erection of the present church, a wooden church had stood on the same spot. It was Father Ranzinger who had built the wooden church, and who had devoted most of his life to that church and its flock. One night, the wooden church went up in flames. Father Ranzinger's lifework was destroyed. I suspect that it is his ghost that has been seen.

After a while I was able to convince the croatian priest who had admitted me to the church, that I meant no harm to the reputation and good name of the church and this particular order of priests, but that I was only interested in writing about natural psychic phenomena, which, after all, are part of God's world. Father X, as he insisted on being called, readily admitted that I was telling the truth and with a somewhat enigmatic smile, he admitted that he, too, had had psychic experiences all his life. As we went on talking, he admitted further that he had seen the ghost of the departed priest himself as had a painter who had been employed in the building to restore the magnificent frescoes put there years before.

Strangely enough, the only one other than myself who wrote anything at all about the haunted church at Millvale was none other than the famous Yugoslav author Louis Adamic, a self-confessed agnostic, a man who does not believe in God. As for the ghostly priest at the altar, he must still be there, roaming the church at will. In view of the difficulties of getting into the church in the first place, I was unable to bring a medium there to attempt a release of the unhappy priest. Thus, my friends, if you happen to be near Pittsburgh and feel like visiting the haunted church of Millvale, and if the time is just right, perhaps at dusk or at dawn, you may just encounter the restless ghost of Father Ranzinger. That is, if he hasn't long since faded away and come to peace with himself, as well he should.

18

Lincoln's Ghost
Washington, D.C.

That Abraham Lincoln would have excellent cause to haunt his former center of activity, even though he died across town, is obvious: he had so much unfinished business of great importance.

Furthermore, Lincoln himself, during his lifetime, had on the record shown an unusual interest in the psychic. The Lincoln family later vehemently denied that séances took place in the White House during his administration. Robert Lincoln may have burned some important papers of his father's bearing on these sittings, along with those concerning the political plot to assassinate his father. According to the record, he most certainly destroyed many documents before being halted in this foolish enterprise by a Mr. Young. This happened shortly before Robert Lincoln's death and is attested to by Lincoln authority Emanuel Hertz in *The Hidden Lincoln*.

The spiritualists even go so far as to claim the President as one of their own. This may be extending the facts, but Abraham Lincoln was certainly psychic, and even during his term in the White House his interest in the occult was well known. The Cleveland *Plain Dealer*, about to write of Lincoln's interest in this subject, asked the President's permission to do so, or, if he preferred, to deny the statements made in the article linking him to these activities. Far from denying it, Lincoln replied, "The only falsehood in the statement is that half of it has not been told. The article does not begin to tell the things I have witnessed."

The séances held in the White House may well have started when Lincoln's little boy Willie followed another son, Eddie, into premature death, and Mrs. Lincoln's mind gave way to a state of temporary insanity. Perhaps to soothe her feelings, Lincoln decided to hold séances in the White house. It is not known whether the results were positive or not, but Willie's ghost has also been seen in the White House. During Grant's administration, according to Arthur Krock, a boy whom they recognized as the apparition of little Willie "materialized" before the eyes of some of his household.

The medium Lincoln most frequently used was one Nettie Colburn Maynard, and allegedly the spirit of Daniel Webster communicated with him through her. On that occasion, it is said, he was urged to proclaim the emancipation of the slaves. That proclamation, as everybody knows, became Lincoln's greatest political achievement. What is less known is the fact that it also laid the foundation for later dissension among his cabinet members and that, as we shall see, it may indirectly have caused his premature death. Before going into this, however, let us make clear that on the whole Lincoln apparently did not need any mediums, for he himself had the gift of clairvoyance, and this talent stayed with him all his life. One of the more remarkable premonitory experiences is reported by Philip Van Doren Stern in *The Man Who Killed Lincoln*, and also in most other sources dealing with Lincoln.

It happened in Springfield in 1860, just after Lincoln had been elected. As he was looking at himself in a mirror, he suddenly saw a double image of himself. One, real and life-like, and an etheric double, pale and shadowy. He was convinced that it meant he would get through his first term safely, but would die before the end of the second. Today, psychic researchers would explain Lincoln's mirror experience in less fanciful terms. What the President saw was a brief "out-of-the-body experience," or astral projection, which is not an uncommon psychic experience. It merely means that the bonds between conscious mind and the unconscious are temporarily loosened and that the inner or true self has quickly slipped out. Usually, these experiences take place in the dream state, but there are cases on record where the phenomenon occurs while awake.

The President's *interpretation* of the experience is of course another matter; here we have a second phenomenon come into play, that of divination; in his peculiar interpretation of his experience, he showed a degree of precognition, and future events, unfortunately, proved him to be correct.

This was not, by far, the only recorded dream experienced in Lincoln's life. He put serious stock in dreams and often liked to interpret them. William Herndon, Lincoln's onetime law partner and biographer, said of him that he always contended he was doomed to a sad fate, and quotes the President as saying many times, "I am sure I shall meet with some terrible end."

It is interesting to note also that Lincoln's fatalism made him often refer to Brutus and Caesar, explaining the events of Caesar's assassination as caused by laws over which neither had any control; years later, Lincoln's murderer, John Wilkes Booth, also thought of himself as the new Brutus slaying the American Caesar because destiny had singled him out for the deed!

Certainly the most widely quoted psychic experience of Abraham Lincoln was a strange dream he had a few days before his death. When his strangely thoughtful mien gave Mrs. Lincoln cause to worry, he finally admitted that he had been disturbed by an unusually detailed dream. Urged, over dinner, to confide his dream, he did so in the presence of Ward Hill Lamon, close friend and social secretary as well as a kind of bodyguard. Lamon wrote it down immediately afterward, and it is contained in his biography of Lincoln: "About ten days ago," the President began, "I retired very late. I had been up waiting for important dispatches from the front. I could not have been long in bed when I fell into a slumber, for I was weary. I soon began to dream. There seemed to be a death-like stillness about me. Then I heard subdued sobs, as if a number of people were weeping. I thought I left my bed and wandered downstairs. There the silence was broken by the same pitiful sobbing, but the mourners were invisible. I went from room to room; no living person was in sight, but the same mournful sounds of distress met me as I passed along. It was light in all the rooms; every object was familiar to me; but where were all the people who were grieving as if their hearts would break? I was puzzled and alarmed. What could be the meaning of all this? Determined to find the cause of a state of things so mysterious and so shocking, I kept on until I arrived at the East Room, which I entered.

"There I met with a sickening surprise. Before me was a catafalque, on which rested a corpse wrapped in funeral vestments. Around it were stationed soldiers who were acting as guards; and there was a throng of people, some gazing mournfully upon the corpse, whose face was covered, others weeping pitifully.

"Who is dead in the White House?" I demanded of one of the soldiers. "The President," was his answer; 'he was killed by an assassin!" Then there came a loud burst of grief from the crowd, which awoke me from my dream. I slept no more that night. . . ."

Lincoln always knew he was a marked man, not only because of his own psychic hunches, but objectively, for he kept a sizable envelope in his desk containing all the threatening letters he had received. That envelope was simply marked "Assassination," and the matter did not frighten him. A man in his position is always in danger, he would argue, although the Civil War and the larger question of what to do with the South after victory had split the country into two factions, making the President's position even more vulnerable. Lincoln, therefore, did not take his elaborate dream warning seriously, or at any rate, he pretended not to. When his friends remonstrated with him, asking him to take extra precautions, he shrugged off their warnings with the lighthearted remark, "Why, it wasn't me on that catafalque. It was some other fellow!"

But the face of the corpse had been covered in his dream and he really was whistling in the dark.

Had Fate wanted to prevent the tragedy and given him warning to avoid it?

Had an even higher order of things decided that he was to ignore that warning?

Lincoln had often had a certain recurrent dream in which he saw himself on a strange ship, moving with great speed toward an indefinite shore. The dream had always preceded some unusual event. In effect, he had dreamed it precisely in the same way preceding the events at Fort Sumter, the battles of Bull Run, Antietam, Gettysburg, Stone River, Vicksburg, and Wilmington. Now he had just dreamed it again on the eve of his death. This was the 13th of April, 1865, and Lincoln spoke of his recurrent dream in unusually optimistic tones. To him it was an indication of impending good news. That news, he felt, would be word from General Sherman that hostilities had ceased. There was a Cabinet meeting scheduled for April 14 and Lincoln hoped the news would come in time for it. It never occurred to him that the important news hinted at by this dream was his own demise that very evening, and that the strange vessel carrying him to a distant shore was Charon's boat ferrying him across the Styx into the nonphysical world.

But had he really crossed over?

Rumors of a ghostly President in the White House kept circulating. They were promptly denied by the government, as would be expected. President Theodore Roosevelt, according to Bess Furman in *White House Profile*, often fancied that he felt Lincoln's spirit, and during the administration of Franklin D. Roosevelt in the 1930s, a girl secretary saw the figure of Abraham Lincoln in his onetime bedroom. The ghost was seated on the bed, pulling on his boots, as if he were in a hurry to go somewhere. This happened in mid-afternoon. Eleanor Roosevelt had often felt Lincoln's presence and freely admitted it.

Now it had been the habit of the administration to put important visitors into what was formerly Lincoln's bedroom. This was not done out of mischief, but merely because the Lincoln room was among the most impressive rooms the White House contained. We have no record of all those who slept there and had eerie experiences, for people, especially politically highly placed people, don't talk with such things as ghosts.

Yet, the late Queen Wilhelmina of the Netherlands did mention the constant knockings at her door followed by footsteps—only to find the corridor outside deserted. And Margaret Truman, who also slept in that area of the White House often heard knocking at her bedroom door at 3 A.M. Whenever she checked, there was nobody there. Her father, President Truman, a skeptic, decided that the noises had to be due to "natural" causes, such as the dangerous settling of the floors. He ordered the White House completely rebuilt, and perhaps this was a good thing. It would surely have collapsed soon after, according to the architect, General Edgerton. Thus, if nothing else, the ghostly knockings had led to a survey of the structure and subsequent rebuilding. Or was that the reason for the knocks? Had Lincoln tried to warn the later occupants that the house was about to fall down around their ears?

Not only Lincoln's bedroom, but other old areas of the White House are evidently haunted. There is, first of all, the famous East Room, where the lying in state took place. By a strange quirk of fate, President Kennedy also was placed there after his assassination. Lynda Bird Johnson's room happened to be the room in which Willie Lincoln died, and later on, Truman's mother. It was also the room used by the doctors to perform the autopsy on Abraham Lincoln. It is therefore not too surprising that President Johnson's daughter did not sleep too well in the room. She heard footsteps at night, and the phone would ring and no one would be on the other end. An exasperated White House telephone operator would come on again and again, explaining she did not ring her!

But if Abraham Lincoln's ghost roams the White House because of unfinished business, it is apparently a ghost free to do other things as well, something the average specter can't do, since it is tied only to the place of its untimely demise.

Mrs. Lincoln lived on for many more years, but ultimately turned senile and died, not in her right mind, at the home of her sister. Long before she became unbalanced, however, she journeyed to Boston in a continuing search for some proof of her late husband's survival of bodily death. This was in the 1880s, and word had reached her that a certain photographer named William Mumler had been able to obtain the likenesses of dead people on his photographic plates under strict test conditions. She decided to try this man, fully aware that fraud might be attempted if she were recognized. Heavily veiled in mourning clothes, she sat down along with other visitors in Mumler's experimental study. She gave the name of Mrs. Tyndall; all Mumler could see was a widow in heavy veils. Mumler then proceeded to take pictures of all those present in the room. When they were developed, there was one of "Mrs. Tyndall." In back of her appears a semi-solid figure of Abraham Lincoln, with his hands resting upon the shoulders of his widow, and an expression of great compassion on his face. Next to Lincoln was the figure of their son Willie, who had died so young in the White House. Mumler showed his prints to the assembled group, and before Mrs. Lincoln could claim her print, another woman in the group exclaimed, "Why, that looks like President Lincoln!" Then Mrs. Lincoln identified herself for the first time.

There is no photograph in existence showing Lincoln with his son in the manner in which they appeared on the psychic photograph.

19

The Ghosts at the Octagon
Washington, D.C.

One of the best known and most beautiful public monuments in the nation's capital is the so-called Octagon, a house built at the beginning of the nineteenth century in octagonal shape, thus its name. Today it is the seat of the offices of the American Institute of Architects and is maintained as a museum. It can be visited but I would advise you

not to stress the ghosts as much as the fact that it is an historical landmark.

Originally built by orders of Colonel John Tayloe in the year 1800 as his townhouse in the new capital, the mansion stands in one of the most fashionable parts of Washington at the corner of New York Avenue and 18th Street. Originally it was surrounded by empty land, but today it forms the center of several avenues of mansions and expensive town houses. The Octagon has three stories and the downstairs part boasts a magnificent rotunda from where a staircase leads to the second and third floors. This particular staircase is the center of ghostly activities in the mansion.

Most of the reported and witnessed phenomena took place on the second floor landing near the banister, on the third floor, and on the ground floor where a carpet keeps flinging itself back where there is no one about. Even before it was finished General Washington spent time in it and during the British occupation of the nation's capital, when the White House had been burned down by the British, the Octagon served as a temporary White House for President Madison and his wife Dolley. It was here that Madison signed a peace treaty with Britain in 1815.

After the death of Mrs. John Tayloe in 1855, the building passed into other hands and was for a time used as a school for girls. But as the neighborhood deteriorated, gradually it became a slum building. It was rescued from its unfortunate state in 1899 when the American Institute of Architects bought it and made it its headquarters.

Ghostly phenomena had been reported from the Octagon as far back as the middle nineteenth century and include footsteps, the sound of a plaintive female voice, and other unusual signs of human presences in the old mansion when no one was seen. A long list of observers have experienced psychic phenomena in the building. Of particular interest is the account of the superintendent Alric H. Clay who has on several occasions found the lights in the building on, after he had just turned all the switches off; on returning, he found the doors wide open where he had just locked them a few minutes before! On one occasion, Mr. Clay was in the basement turning the switches off again, having been summoned to the house by the police in the middle of the night, when he clearly heard footsteps in an area he had just visited a minute before. The shock was too much for the superintendent: he almost electrocuted himself at the switches, then quickly ran up stairs only to find himself again alone in the building.

The footsteps of both a man and a woman have been heard repeatedly by witnesses, especially on the second and third floors. A carpet at the bottom of the main staircase keeps flinging itself back when there is no one in the building. This is a spot immediately to the right of the staircase in the center of the downstairs hall. The chandeliers also swing of their own volition at times.

Once the assistant curator heard footsteps on the third floor when she was working on the second floor. Knowing full well that the third floor had been closed to visitors and in fact had been shut off altogether for a long time, she was puzzled as to who might be walking up and down over her head. She then tiptoed up to the third floor and looked around. There was no one to be seen, but in the dust of the floor she noticed some very light footprints, far too light to have been made by human feet and yet indicating the outlines of two delicate feet belonging to an unseen woman.

I visited the Octagon several times, twice in the company of a competent medium. The reason for the haunting goes back to the original builder of the house, stern Colonel John Tayloe. It appears that one of his daughters had fallen in love with the wrong kind of man and Colonel Tayloe would have no part of it. The daughter then commited suicide by jumping from the second floor landing. She fell and broke her neck on the very spot where the carpet keeps flinging itself back by its own volition. However, this would not account for the heavy footsteps clearly belonging to a man. These are thought to be of Colonel Tayloe himself, the distraught father who had indirectly caused his daughter's death. There may, however, be a third ghost in the Octagon.

During the British occupation period a young officer pursued one of the American servant girls who preferred to jump to her death rather than give in to his demands. We don't have her name, but visitors often report someone standing behind them on the upper floor where the servants slept. No attempt at exorcising any of these ghosts was made by me, so for all I know they may still be roaming the corridors of the Octagon.

20

Haunted Fort McNair,
Washington D.C.

Fort McNair is one of the oldest military posts in the United States and has had many other names. First it was known as the Arsenal, then called the Washington Arsenal, and in 1826 a penitentiary was built on its grounds, which was a grim place indeed. President Lincoln, because of the horrible conditions there, ordered the penitentiary closed in 1862, but as soon as Lincoln had been murdered, the penitentiary was back in business again.

Among the conspirators accused of having murdered President Lincoln, the one innocent person was Mrs. Mary Suratt, whose sole crime consisted of having run a boarding house where her son had met with some of the conspirators. But her son, John Suratt, was actually a double-agent, so the irony is even greater.

She was the first woman hanged in the United States, and today historians are fully convinced that she was totally innocent. The trial itself was conducted in a most undemocratic manner, and it is clear in retrospect that the conspirators never had a chance. But the real power behind the Lincoln assassination, who might have been one of his own political associates, wanted to make sure no one was left who knew anything abut the ploy, and so Mary Suratt had to be sacrificed.

There is a small, ordinary looking building called Building 21 at Ft. McNair, not far from what is now a pleasant tennis court. It was in this building that Mary Suratt was imprisoned and to this day sobs are heard in the early hours of the morning by a number of people quartered in the building. The penitentiary stands no more, the land itself is now part of the tennis court. Next to Building 21 is an even smaller house, which serves as quarters for a number of officers.

When I visited the post a few years ago, the Deputy Post Commander was quartered there. Building 20 contains five apartments which were remodeled a few years ago. The ceilings have been lowered, the original wooden floors have been replaced with asbestos tile. Unexplained fires occurred there in the mid 1960s. The execution of the conspirators, including Mrs. Mary Suratt, took place just a few yards from where Building 21 now stands. The graves of the hanged conspirators were in what is now the tennis court, but the coffins were removed a few years after the trial and there are no longer any bodies in the ground.

Captain X.—and his name must remain secret for obvious reasons—had lived in apartment Number 5 for several years prior to my interviewing him. He has not heard the sobbing of Mary Suratt but he has heard a strange sound, like high wind.

However, Captain and Mrs. X. occupied quarters on the third floor of Building 20 for several years until 1972. This building, incidentally, is the only part of the former penitentiary still standing. The X.'s apartment consisted of the entire third floor and it was on this floor that the conspirators, including John Wilkes Booth, who was already dead, were tried and sentenced to die by hanging. Mary Suratt's cell was also located on the third floor of the building. Mrs. X. has had ESP experiences before, but she was not quite prepared for what occurred to her when she moved onto the post at Ft. McNair.

"My experiences in our apartment at Ft. McNair were quite unlike any other I have ever known." On several occasions, very late at night, someone could be heard walking above, yet we were on the top floor. One night the walking became quite heavy, and a window in the room which had been Mrs. Suratt's cell was continually being rattled as if someone were trying to get in or out, and there seemed to be a

definite presence in the house. This happened in April, as did the trial of the conspirators.

    I doubt that it would be easy to visit Ft. McNair for any except official reasons, such as perhaps an historical investigation. But for better or for worse, the building in question is located on the northeast corner of the tennis courts and Ft. McNair itself is in Washington, D.C., at the corner of Fourth and P Street and easy to reach from the center of the city.

21

The Ghostly Rocking Chair
Ash Lawn, Virginia

Not only houses are haunted, even furniture can be the recipient of ghostly attention. Not very far from Castle Hill, Virginia, is one of America's most important historical buildings, the country home once owned by James Monroe, where he and Thomas Jefferson often exchanged conversa-

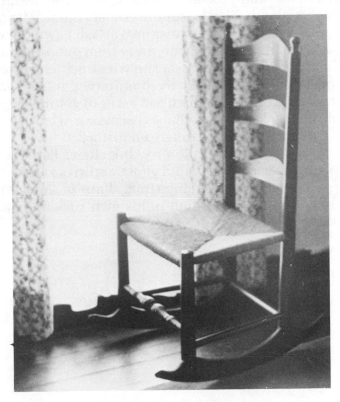

tion, and also may have made some very big political decisions in their time. It is a modest-appearing, well-kept cottage, which can be visited by tourists at certain hours, since it is considered an historical shrine.

The ghostly happenings center around a certain wooden rocking chair in the main room. This has been seen to rock without benefit of human hands. I don't know how many people have actually seen the chair rock, but Mrs. Joseph Massey, who lived in the area for many years, has said to me when I visited the place, "I will tell anyone and I have no objection to its being known, that I've seen not once but time and time again that chair rocking exactly as though someone were in it. My brother John has seen it too. Whenever we touched it it would stop rocking."

This house, small and cozy as it was and is, nevertheless, was James Monroe's favorite house even after he moved to the bigger place which became his stately home later on in his career. Perhaps it was because here at Ash Lawn he could get away from his affairs of state, away from public attention and discuss matters of great concern with his friend Thomas Jefferson. After all, Jefferson lived only two miles away at Monticello and the two of them had a way of getting together through the back roads, perhaps discussing what later became an important part of American history.

Who is the ghost in the rocking chair? Perhaps it is only a spirit, not an earth-bound ghost, a spirit so attached to his former home, once his refuge from affairs of state, that he still likes to sit now and then in his own rocking chair to think things over.

22

Haunted Michie Tavern
Virginia

Michie Tavern is one of the best known attractions in historic Charlottesville, Virginia. "This typical pre-Revolutionary tavern was a favorite stopping place for travelers," the official guide to Charlottesville says. "With its Colonial furniture and china, its beamed and paneled rooms, it appears much the way it did in the days when Jefferson and Monroe were visitors. Monroe writes of entertaining Lafayette as his guest at dinner here, and General Andrew Jackson, fresh from his victory at New Orleans, stopped over on his way to Washington."

The guide, however, does not mention that the tavern was moved a considerable distance from its original place to a much more accessible location where the tourist trade could benefit from it more. Regardless of this comparatively recent change of position, the tavern is exactly as it was, with everything inside, including its ghosts, intact. At the original site, it was surrounded by trees which framed it and sometimes towered over it. At the new site, facing the road, it looks out into the Virginia countryside almost like a manor house.

One walks up to the wooden structure over a number of steps and enters the old tavern to the left or, if one prefers, the pub to the right, which is nowadays a coffee shop. Taverns in the eighteenth and early nineteenth centuries were not simply bars or inns; they were meeting places where people could talk freely, sometimes about political subjects. They were used as headquarters for revolutionary movements or for invading military forces. Most taverns of any size had ballrooms in which the social functions of the

area could be held. Only a few private individuals were wealthy enough to have their own ballrooms built into their manor houses.

What is fortunate about Michie Tavern is the fact that everything is pretty much as it was in the eighteenth century, and whatever restorations have been undertaken are completely authentic. I visited the allegedly haunted tavern in the company of Virginia Cloud, who lives in Charlottesville, and my psychic friend Ingrid Beckman, for whom this was a first visit to Charlottesville. Horace Burr, the eminent historian and art collector, was also one of the party.

Ingrid kept looking into various rooms, sniffing out the psychic presences, as it were, while I followed close behind. Horace and Virginia kept a respectable distance, as if trying not to "frighten" the ghosts away. That was alright with me, because I did not want Ingrid to tap the unconscious mind of either one of these very knowledgeable people.

Finally, we arrived in the third-floor ballroom of the old tavern. I asked Ingrid what she had felt in the various rooms below. "In the pink room on the second floor I felt an argument or some sort of strife, but nothing special in any of the other rooms. I'm impressed with an argument over a woman here," Ingrid continued. "It has to do with one of the dignitaries, and it is about one of their wives."

"How does the argument end?"

"I think they just had a quick argument here, about her infidelity."

"Who are the people involved?"

"I think Hamilton. I don't know the woman's name."

"Who is the other man?"

"I think Jefferson was here."

"Try to get as much of the argument as you can."

Ingrid closed her eyes, sat down in a chair generally off-limits to visitors, and tried to tune in on the past. "I get the argument as a real embarrassment," she began. "The woman is frail, she has a long dress on with lace at the top part around the neck, her hair is light brown."

"Does she take part in the argument?"

"Yes, she has to side with her husband."

"Describe her husband."

"I can't see his face, but he is dressed in a brocade jacket pulled back with buttons down the front and breeches. It is a very fancy outfit."

"How does it all end?"

"Well, nothing more is said. It is just a terrible embarrassment."

"Is this some sort of special occasion? Are there other people here?"

"Yes, oh yes. It is like an anniversary or something of that sort. Perhaps a political anniversary of some kind. There is music and dancing and candlelight."

Horace wasn't sure what it could have been, but Virginia, in great excitement, broke in here. "It was in this room that the waltz was danced for the first time in America. A young man dressed in fancy clothes had come from France. The lady he danced with was a closely chaperoned girl from Charlottesville. She was very young, and she danced the waltz with this young man, and everybody in Charlottesville was shocked. The news went around town that the young lady had danced with a man holding her, and that was just terrible at the time. Perhaps that was the occasion."

So if you feel like visiting Michie Tavern, you may or may not run into the lively party upstairs in the ballroom, but then these are fairly happy ghosts even if they shocked their contemporaries at the time.

23

The Haunting in the Postmaster's House
Virginia

One of the most charming and at the same time historically important houses in Charlottesville, Virginia, nowadays serves as the home of Mr. Beagle, the local postmaster, a
man fully aware of the history all around him, who has taken
excellent care of the old house. The house is known locally
simply as "the Farm." Actually, it is a handsome two-story
brick house, with a prominent fireplace on one end. The
downstairs is now divided into two rooms—a front room
very much the way it was in Colonial days, and a back room
now used by the owner as a kind of storage room. Upstairs are
two bedrooms. The house stands in a tree-studded lot right in
the very center of Charlottesville. A little to the left of the
house the postmaster pointed out the spot where the King's
old Highway used to go through.

On the outside of the Farm, a simple plaque reminds
visitors that this is one of the most historical spots in the area.
Carefully avoiding any opportunity for my medium friend
Ingrid Beckman to see that plaque, historian Horace Burr,
local expert Virginia Cloud, Ingrid, and I arrived at the Farm
at three o'clock in the afternoon and immediately proceeded
to the main room downstairs, where Ingrid stood transfixed
in front of the Colonial fireplace.

"I have the feeling that wounded people are being
brought in right down here," Ingrid said. "I get the name
Langdon or Langley and the name Nat." She walked around
the room and then returned to her position near the fireplace.
"I think the people with the light-colored breeches and the
brown waistcoats and the long rifles are watching the road

nearby for someone to come up that road. This is like a blockhouse, and there is some great anxiety about someone on his way up here. This is a last-ditch defense; there are perhaps five or six men, and they are upstairs with those huge rifles pointing with their long barrels and bayonets on top of them. The bullets are homemade, and it is the middle of the night. And then I get the feeling of a skirmish."

I turned to Horace Burr, asking him to comment on our observations. He seemed plainly delighted. "Well, I thought the most amazing thing that you said was this kind of replay of a group of armed forces, a flank because there was a very interesting little maneuver that happened down the road, an attempt to cut off the main body of the British armed forces coming here. The attempt went awry, though. The American troops were entrenched along the road here, expecting the British to come *this* way. Unfortunately, they came the *other* way, so the British did take Charlottesville for one night."

"What about the name Nat?"

"This house was owned at the time by Nicholas Merriweather Lewis. He was a colonel and George Washington's aide. Nat was a colonial nickname for Nicholas."

It was on June 14, 1781, that Colonel Banastre Tarleton, the British commander, had been seen by John Jouett, who then took his famous ride to warn Jefferson and the legislature of the approaching British. When Tarleton finally got to Charlottesville late the same day, proceeding along the old King's Highway and destroying several wagonloads of Continental supplies on the way, he thwarted the carefully laid plans of the defenders of Charlottesville, 200 men to whom the defense of the village had been entrusted. They had been planning an ambush in the gorge below Monticello.

Captain John Marson, in command of the detachment, was disappointed, but there was nothing to be done. As Tarleton entered Charlottesville, he saw the Farm, with Mrs. Lewis standing at the door, far more curious than frightened. "I think maybe I'll stay here," Tarleton is quoted as saying, and decided to make the Farm his headquarters for the night.

Mrs. Lewis had heard all sorts of stories about the handsome Tarleton. The Colonel was 27 and very courteous. "Madam, you dwell in a little paradise," she quoted him in her dairy.

Tarleton spent the night in front of the fireplace which had so attracted Ingrid, leaving the rest of the house to Mrs. Lewis, whose husband was away with the Continental Army.

I doubt that the ghost of Colonel Tarleton is still in the postmaster's house, but anyone lucky enough to visit there might pick up a psychic impression from the past. If there are ghosts in the house, they are not the Colonel's, but perhaps some of the wounded who might have died during the skirmish between the two sides. At any rate, this is a private house and permission must be obtained from the gracious postmaster to visit.

24

Jefferson's Spirit at Monticello, Virginia

There's hardly any need to explain who Thomas Jefferson was, but perhaps there should be some light shed on the curious interest our present day historians have in him. Much new material about his private life has lately come to light, and the architect of the Declaration of Independence does seem to have had his more human side as well as his patriotic image.

Monticello, which every schoolboy knows from its representation on the American five-cent piece, is probably one of the finest examples of American architecture. It was designed by Jefferson himself, who lies buried here in the family graveyard. It stands on a hill looking down into the valley of Charlottesville, perhaps 15 minutes from the town proper. Carefully landscaped grounds surround the house.

Inside, the house is laid out in classical proportions. From the entrance hall with its famous clock, also designed by Jefferson, one enters a large, round room, the heart of the house. On both sides of this central area are rectangular rooms. To the left is a corner room, used as a study and library from where Jefferson, frequently early in the morning before anyone else was up, used to look out on the rolling hills of Virginia. Adjacent to it is a very small bedroom, almost a bunk.

Thus, the entire west wing of the building is a self-contained apartment in which Jefferson could be active without interfering with the rest of his family. On the other side of the round central room is a large dining room leading

to a terrace which, in turn, continues into an open walk with a magnificent view of the hillside. The furniture is Jefferson's own, as are the silver and china, some of it returned to Monticello in recent years by history-conscious citizens of the area who had purchased it in various ways.

But it was the little honeymoon cottage behind the main house that attracted my psychic friend, Ingrid Beckman, more than other rooms in the main house. Built in the same classical American style as Monticello itself, the building contains two fair-sized rooms, on two stories. A walk leads to the entrance to the upper story, barricaded by an iron grillwork to keep the tourists out. After a while I turned to Ingrid, asking her what impressions she received from the honeymoon cottage.

"Well, I think the wife was not living on her level, her standard, and she was unhappy. It wasn't what she was used to. It wasn't grand enough. I think she had doubts about him and his plans."

"In what sense?"

"I think she was dubious about what would happen. She was worried that he was getting too involved, and she didn't like his political affiliations too well."

I turned to my other companion, Horace Burr, an historian and art collector, for comments. To my surprise, Horace asked me to turn off my tape recorder since the information was of a highly confidential nature. However, he pointed out that the material could be found in *American Heritage*, and that I was free to tell the story in my own words.

Apparently, there had always been a problem between Jefferson and his wife concerning other women. His associations were many and varied. All this did not contribute to Mrs. Jefferson's happiness. Gossip and legend intermingle in small towns and in the countryside. This is especially true when important historical figures are involved.

Could it be that part of Thomas Jefferson still clings to this little cottage where he found much happiness? A visit with Mr. Jefferson, one way or another, should prove rewarding if only for historical reasons. But then one never knows, if the visitor is psychic, what might happen.

25

Westover's Evelyn,
Virginia

Foremost among Virginia manor houses is the magnificent estate of Westover on the James River. Built originally in 1730 by William Byrd II, the man who founded Richmond, it stands amid an 11,000-acre working farm. The formal gardens surrounding the house in the entrance hall match the paneling of the walls. Throughout the manor house there is evidence of grandeur. This is not the home of a country squire, but of a statesman of great wealth.

After William Byrd was killed during the Revolutionary War, the widow sold the original furniture. Eventually the house passed into the hands of Mrs. Bruce Crane Fisher. Her grandfather had bought the house in 1921 and became the eleventh owner since the plantation had been in existence. Mrs. Fisher furnished the house in recent years with authentic eighteenth-century English and European furniture to restore it as closely as possible to the original appearance.

The Georgian house stands amid tall old trees and consists of a central portion and two wings. The central portion has three stories of elegant brickwork and two tall chimneys. The two wings were originally not connected to the center portion of the house, but the right wing had to be restored in 1900 since it had been damaged by fire from a shelling during the Civil War. At that time the two wings were also connected to the house and are now accessible directly from the main portion. The main entrance faces the James River and has the original wrought-iron entrance gate with stone eagles surmounting the gate-posts. Thus, with minimal additions and restorations, the house today presents pretty much the same picture it did when it was first built in 1730.

Colonel Byrd took his beautiful daughter Evelyn (pronounced "Eevelyn" in Virginia) to London for the coronation of King George I. That was in 1717 when the great men of the colonies, if they could afford it, would come to the mother country when the occasion arose. Evelyn, at the time, was 18 years old and her father decided to leave her in England to be educated. Soon he received disquieting news from his confidants at the London court. It appeared that Evelyn had been seen with a certain Charles Mordaunt and that the two young people were desperately in love with each other. Normally this would be a matter for rejoicing, but not so in this case. Charles was an ardent Roman Catholic and the grandson of the Earl of Peterborough. Colonel Byrd, on the other hand, was politically and personally a staunch Protestant, and the idea of his daughter marrying into the enemy camp, so to speak, was totally unacceptable to him. Immediately he ordered her to return to Westover, and Evelyn had no choice but to obey. As soon as she arrived at the family plantation she went into isolation. She refused to see any other suitors her father sent her or to consider, or even to discuss, the possibility of marriage.

This went on for some time, and Evelyn quite literally "pined away" to death. Some weeks before her death, however, she had a very emotional discussion with her best friend, Anne Harrison. The two girls were walking up a hill when Evelyn, feeling faint, knew that her days were numbered. She turned to her friend and promised her that she would return after her death. Mrs. Harrison did not take this very seriously, but she knew that Evelyn was not well and her death did not come as a shock.

The following spring, after Westover had somehow returned to a degree of normalcy and the tragic events of the previous year were not so strongly in evidence, Mrs. Harrison was walking in the garden, sadly remembering what had transpired the year before. Suddenly she saw her old friend standing beside her in a dazzling white gown. The vision then drifted forward two steps, waved its hand at her and smiled. An instant later it vanished. At the time of her untimely death Evelyn Byrd had been 29 years of age, but in the apparition she seemed much younger and lovelier than she had appeared toward the end of her life. The specter has reappeared from time to time to a number of people, both those who live in the area and those who are guests at Westover.

A lady who lives nearby, who has been there for nearly three decades, saw her in the mid 1960s. She had been coming out of the front door one summer day and was walking down the path when she looked back toward the house and saw a woman come out behind her. At first she thought it was a friend and stopped at the gate to wait for her. When the woman came closer, however, she didn't recognize her. There was something very strange about the woman coming toward her. There seemed to be a glow all about her person, her black hair, and the white dress. When the woman had arrived close to her, she stopped and seemed to sink into the ground.

On December 11, 1929, some guests from Washington were staying at Westover and on the evening of their arrival the conversation turned to ghosts. The house was then owned by Mr. and Mrs. Richard H. Crane, who explained that they themselves had not seen the ghost during their tenancy. One of the house guests retired to the room assigned to her on the side of the house overlooking the great gates, from which one has a fine view into the formal gardens. Sometime that night the guest awoke and went to the window. There was no apparent reason for her behavior. It was quite dark outside and very quiet. As she glanced out the window, she saw the figure of Evelyn Byrd. She described the apparition to her hosts as filmy, nebulous and cloudy, so transparent that no features could be distinguished, only a gauzy texture of a woman's form. The figure seemed to be floating a little above the lawn and almost on the level of the window itself. As she looked at it, almost transfixed, the apparition acknowledged her by raising her hand and motioning to her to go back into the room and away from the window. The gesture seemed so imperative that the house guest obeyed it.

26

The Howard Mansion
Texas

The old Howard home on South Main Street in Henderson, Texas, is a Southern mansion of the kind that is so numerous throughout the South. In 1851 the mansion was erected by a certain James L. Howard on land he paid $100 for. It is the oldest brick home in town. Today it belongs to the Heritage Association and is being maintained as a museum, with visitors coming not only from other parts of Texas but even from abroad. The house has three stories and six rooms. Four columns adorn its front. Perhaps the most remarkable thing about the house is the fact that every room has a fireplace, some of them very large, old-fashioned fireplaces of the kind you rarely see any more. The stairs have banisters made of the highest grade walnut.

When the Howards built this home they stated proudly, to anyone who would hear it, "God Almighty Himself could not tear it down because it was so well built." Even the worst storm seemingly could not touch the house. There is an account of a particularly horrifying electrical storm when a streak of lightning hit one of the corner columns, causing only slight damage. One of the Howard brothers ran out into the yard, looked up into the sky and shook his fist and said, "See, I told you that you couldn't tear down my house."

With so large and outstanding a mansion in a small town, it is only natural that legends would crop up around it, some of which are true and some not. One of them making the rounds concerns a murder in the house. The present owners, the Rusk Company Heritage Association, has checked into it and found that an accident and not a murder had occurred. The accident concerns a member of the Howards named Pat Howard, who lost his life under mysterious circumstances. In fact, the descendants of the Howards went to great lengths to explain again and again that Pat Howard died of an accident and that the shooting that took his life was not murder in any sense of the word. Of course where there is smoke there is sometimes fire. Was the family merely trying to kill the story, or were they correcting the facts?

In 1905 Mrs. A.A. Howard and Dore Howard, being childless, decided to sell the house to a certain Mrs. M.A. Dickinson. Mrs. Howard was then in ill health. The sale did not go down well with her and the rest of the family, who would have preferred to have the house remain as family property. It seems incredible today that such an imposing house could be sold for $1,500, but of course that was a lot more money in 1905 than it is today. Still, even for 1905, $1,500 was very little money for a house of this kind. It seems strange, therefore, that the sale was made in this manner.

The sale of the house from the Howard family to an outsider took the town by surprise. No one had surmised that it could be for sale, especially not for such a low price. The house had a reputation as a historical landmark. Sam Houston himself had slept there many times, since he was a cousin of the Howards. In 1950 the house passed from the Dickinson family to Hobard Bryce, who in 1961 deeded the property to the Historical Association. One of the townspeople who had spent much effort in restoring the old house and who had been active on behalf of the fund-raising committee was a certain Carl Jaggers. Partly due to his efforts and those of others, the house is now in excellent condition again and open to visitors as a museum. My attention was drawn to it when I appeared on a television program in nearby Tyler, Texas. The woman who interviewed me, Jane Lassiter, provided me with much of the material about the Henderson house.

While the controversy among the townspeople concerning the restoration of the house was going on and there
was some doubt whether the house could be saved or had to
be torn down, no one had the time or inclination to look into
any possible ghostly manifestations at the house. But as soon
as the matter had quieted down and the house was safe from
the wreckers' ball and perhaps because of the renewed quiet
in the atmosphere something did occur that had not been
observed before. Maia Jaggers was one of those who served as
honorary guides about the house, particularly during the
weekends when there were more visitors than during the
week. She acted as hostess to those who came to look at the
house. One Sunday afternoon in the winter of 1968, she had
just finished showing the house to a group of visitors and was
quite alone in it for the moment. She found herself downstairs looking toward the stairway leading to the upper
stories. At that precise moment she saw a woman materialize
before her eyes. Seemingly solid, or almost so, it was clearly a
woman of a past age. As she looked closely at the apparition,
she realized that it was the ghost of Mrs. Howard herself. As
soon as Maia Jaggers and the ghost had come face-to-face, the
apparition floated up the stairway and disappeared. She has
not been seen since that time. Could it be that a grateful Mrs.
Howard wanted the one person directly connected with the
salvage of her home made aware of her continued existence
in it? Was her presence in what was once her home caused by
a belated regret at having sold out to others against the
wishes of her family? If you are ever in Henderson, Texas be
sure and drop in on Mrs. Howard's house. Sale or no sale, she
seems to be quite at home in it still.

27

The Haunted Nightclub
of Toronto

The Mynah Bird is an unusual nightclub in the York-
ville district of Toronto, Canada, an artistic neighborhood
known for its unusual attractions. The old house is narrow
and has two stories and an attic, or third story, if you wish.
The Mynah Bird nowadays has so-called skin shows, and
occasional "adult movies." Colin Kerr is the owner of this
emporium, which is no worse—in fact, much better—than
most striptease or sex-exploitation-oriented nightclubs in
the United States. The atmosphere is clean, alcohol is not
served, and the audiences are small. The main attractions are
a series of solo dance performances by seminude girls, a
session in body painting (with the customers getting into the
act), and, since the haunting was discovered, an occasional
séance. The latter smacks of commercialism and is not to be
taken too seriously.

The psychic goings-on started when Kerr changed the
club's policy from that of a straight dancing club to the
topless entertainment. Possibly the ghosts objected. Lights
would go on and off at various times—mostly off, as if someone were trying to put a halt to the proceedings.

At first, the manager paid no attention to these reports. Partly he doubted that anything unusual was going on
and partly because he felt that such strange phenomena, if
they were genuine, could only enhance the attraction of the
place for tourists.

But soon he had to revise that view. The tourists who
were told that the place might be haunted laughed. They had
come to see bodies, not spirits. It was all the same to them.
But the girls who worked for the club were another matter.

Many came from outlying provinces, little villages, and the backwoods. Their fears were very real. All of a sudden, Kerr noticed that his girls would not stay alone in a certain part of the house, especially upstairs. The turnover of personnel at the Mynah was always considerable and did not worry Kerr. To the contrary, he liked to replace his girls frequently since his customers liked to see new faces—or bodies, for that matter. But he began to realize that some of his new girls quit awfully fast. There was no reason for that, since they were always treated decently, customers never got out of line with them, and Mr. Kerr watched over the shows with a sense of pride rather unusual for the operator of a nightclub. Nevertheless, the turnover continued.

Kerr began to question his girls in a calm, low-key voice concerning unusual phenomena they might have observed. At first, the girls did not like to talk, perhaps out of fear of losing their jobs. On the other hand, the uncanny presences in the club also worried them. Before long, the strange occurrences began to happen with greater frequency and seemed to be more definite in character, as if someone or something wanted to make his or its presence known in a forceful manner. Musical instruments would move from their proper place by themselves. A male presence spoke to Mr. Kerr's father-in-law upstairs, in the area where the "adult movies" were being shown at the time. Chairs were thrown all over the place in the upstairs room when there had been no one about. Kerr discovered that the theatre where the "adult movies" were being shown was originally an artist's studio. One of the girl dancers felt a man standing close to her, whom she could not see—yet she knew he was angry, and she tried to appease the unseen stranger. Another girl working at the club, also psychic, described the entity as an old man with gray hair and a beard. But there may also be a woman ghost on the premises, judging from the smell of perfume that has been observed at times.

The Mynah Bird is open seven evenings a week, and can be visited freely. In addition to the ghostly performances—which cannot be guaranteed—there are the flesh and blood ones you can always count on and they are sufficient reason to visit.

28

Rose Hall, Home of
the "White Witch"
of Jamaica

Sometimes referred to as the most haunted house in the Western Hemisphere, Rose Hall is the great house of Rose Hall Plantation, one of the largest estates of Colonial Jamaica. It has recently been purchased by an American hotelman and meticulously restored to its former glory for use as a hotel for affluent tourists.

The plantation is not far from the Montego Bay airport, and a good road leads up to it. To this day, however, some natives will not go near the house, referring to it as filled with "goopies," a local term for ghosts. They are indeed right. The earthbound spirit of Annie Porter, once mistress of Rose Hall, has never been laid to rest.

I have been to Rose Hall on two occasions, but without a proper trance medium. It is particularly in the corridors beneath the house that stark terror dwells, and I caution anyone visiting Rose Hall to beware of those areas, especially at night.

Annie Porter was a sadistic woman, who first made lovers of some of her more handsome slaves, and then tortured them to death. Eventually, fate caught up with her, and she too was put to death by one of those she had first tormented. Much violence and hatred cling to the old masonry, and are not likely to have disappeared just because the building had some of its holes filled in and painted over.

The house has three stories and a magnificent staircase out front, by which one gains access to the main floor. It is surrounded by trees and some of the most beautiful landscape in Jamaica. Prior to its restoration, it looked the way a haunted house is always described in fiction or film, with empty windows and broken walls. Now, however, it presents a clean and majestic appearance.

Annie Porter is also referred to as "the White Witch of Rose Hall." There are actually two Annie Porters recorded in history and buried in a nearby cemetery. In the popular legend, the two figures have become amalgamated, but it is the Annie Porter of the late British Colonial period who committed the atrocities which force her to remain tied to what was once her mansion. I do not doubt that she is still there.

I base this assumption on solid evidence. About ten years ago the late great medium Eileen Garrett paid Rose Hall a visit in the company of distinguished researchers. Her mission was to seek out and, if possible, appease the restless spirit of Annie Porter. Within a matter of moments after her arrival at the Hall, Mrs. Garrett went into a deep trance. The personality of the terror-stricken ghost took over her body, vocal chords, facial expression, and all, and tried to express the pent-up emotions that had so long been dormant.

The researchers were hard-pressed to follow the entranced Mrs. Garrett from the terrace, where their quest had begun, through half-dilapidated corridors, underground passages, and dangerously undermined rooms. But Annie Porter wanted them to see the places where she had been the Mistress of Rose Hall, reliving through the medium some of her moments of glory.

Eventually, these revived memories led to the point where Annie met her doom at the hand of a young slave with whom she had earlier had an affair.

Crying uncontrollably, writhing on all fours, the medium was by now completely under the control of the restless ghost. No matter how soothingly the researchers spoke to her, asking Annie to let go of the dreadful past, the violent behavior continued. Annie would not leave. In one of the few rare cases on record where a ghost is so tormented and tied to the place of its tragedy that it cannot break away, Annie refused to leave. Instead, the research team left, with a very shaken medium in tow.

V
Haunted Locations, America

29

The Haunted Lady
of Nob Hill
San Francisco, California

On California Street, not far from the Fairmont Hotel, where the cable car stops, there is an intersection flanked by some of the oldest houses in San Francisco. It is here that the ghost of Flora Sommerton walks. Mrs. Gwen Hinzie saw her as recently as 1962. She was riding up California Street in a cable car in the company of a friend. Both ladies, looking out the window, noticed a strange girl walking up the street beside the cable car, wearing what appeared to be an odd dress for the time of day. The dress Mrs. Hinzie described as a kind of ballgown, and what was even more remarkable was the fact that the stranger seemed to walk right through people ahead of her. Others have noticed the lovely young girl seemingly walking straight ahead, as if she was trying to get away from something or someone down the hill.

The case concerned a San Francisco debutante, Flora Sommerton. A few hours before her scheduled debut, 18-year-old Flora disappeared from her mansion on Nob Hill, causing one of the major scandals of the year 1876. Her reason was that she did not care to marry the young man her parents had picked out for her. The girl was never found despite a huge reward offered for her return.

Ever since her disappearance, rumors have circulated that she had been seen here or there, but all of them turned out to be false. For the most part, these were feeble attempts at getting money from Flora's parents. However, as the years went by and the girl did not turn up, the family built a wall of indifference around themselves and Flora was no longer

discussed. The reward was withdrawn. No one who wanted to remain on good terms with the Sommertons dared mention Flora or to ask if anything new about her had turned up.

The parents eventually accepted the medical theory that Flora's mind had snapped under the pressure of pre-wedding excitement. It was better to believe this version than to admit to themselves the real cause of Flora's panic. The man they had wanted her to marry was simply not the man she wanted. Afraid to face her parents in rebellion, she did the only thing she was capable of under the circumstances: she ran away. She did not even wait to change clothes, running up the hill in a ballgown. Truly Flora's action was not premeditated but sudden, and in panic.

When the parents died, even the rumors of Flora's reappearance died out. It was not until much later that her name became once again newsworthy in her native city.

Eventually, Flora died broke and ill in 1926, in a flophouse hotel in Butte, Montana. When found, she was dressed in a white ballgown of the 1880s. It was that same ballgown she was wearing when Mrs. Hinzie saw her ghost walking up Nob Hill with a determined look.

I cannot promise that in today's traffic anyone will notice the unusually clad young lady, but it is just possible that in the still of night and with great patience, a sensitive individual might feel her presence in the area. If you will slowly walk up and down the hill, starting at California Street, perhaps you will be one of the lucky few.

30

Haunted Clinton Court
New York City

Hell's Kitchen is not one of the best neighborhoods of Manhattan. The houses lining the streets generally do not show much charm or artistic invention. Thus, it must come as a great surprise to the casual visitor when he passes by the facade of Number 420 West 46th Street, goes through a narrow lane closed off by an iron gate, and finds himself in a courtyard of great beauty and charm. Across the courtyard is another building, Number 422½ West 46th Street. This is Clinton Court, named after Governor George Clinton whose carriage house it once was. The ground itself was at one time used as a Potter's Field, the cemetery for the poor and for the executed. Consequently, there are "presences" here in various spots, remainders from New York's past, when this area was fairly far "uptown."

When the British ruled New York, one of those buried here was a certain character known locally as "Old Moor," a sailor executed for mutiny.

His ghost was the first phantom seen at this place. In the 1820s, when the house was still used as a carriage house for the estate of Governor Clinton and his family, Old Moor would appear and frighten people. One day he frightened the wife of a coachman, who fell down the winding stairs to her death. These very stairs, leading from the upper story to the ground, still exist, although a second staircase, farther to the rear, has since disappeared. The coachman's wife became ghost number two.

The ghostly legend of the house was so well known that the Clinton children played a private little game called

"Ghosts." One day, one of the Clinton children, frightened by a real apparition, stumbled and fell to her death, becoming ghost number three. This child ghost was seen by the late Ruth Shaw, an artist who had rented the downstairs portion of the carriage house some years ago. All of the hauntings are confined to that part of the building. The front, giving on to 46th Street, has never been affected.

I have held several investigations at this address, including one with Ethel Johnson Meyers and another with Sybil Leek. I have also made a television film about it. Through Sybil I met the ghost of a colonial officer named Walker at 422½ West 46th Street. Enough personal data was received and checked out in regimental records to prove that such a man existed and that, at any rate, the medium could not have known about it. He died in a duel.

While it is not difficult to walk into the courtyard of Clinton Court, as the house is still called, getting access to the

two apartments is another matter. They are privately owned and do not look for visitors—especially not those who come for the ghosts rather than the flesh and blood people. Today the house is divided between two tenants. The family of Leo Herbert, property man for David Merrick, lives upstairs, and the Nearys have the downstairs portion. But since some of the phenomena have actually occurred outside the building, on the winding staircase and in the courtyard itself, it is entirely possible that a sensitive individual might experience *something* outside the apartments. I suggest that one go there at dusk and experience the quietness of the courtyard in contrast to the surrounding street noises. In particular, I suggest a walk up and down those winding stairs. Who knows which one of the four resident ghosts one might encounter?

31

The Haunted Frigate *Constellation*
Baltimore, Maryland

Tied up at the pier in Baltimore and open to the public as a kind of floating museum, is the proud U.S.F. *Constellation*, once the flagship of the American Navy. Built in 1797 as the first man-of-war of the United States fleet, the ship was still in commission as late as World War II. Part of its superstructure has recently been restored, and the timbers are only partially the original wood, but otherwise nothing has been changed. This is important since the hauntings would not continue if most or all of the original material had been replaced.

Congress tried to decommission the U.S.F. *Constellation* several times and to pass her name on to a newer ship. But something would always happen to prevent this, or the new carrier of the name *Constellation* would become the victim of accidents. Gradually, however, the old ship outlived her usefulness, and, despite her heroic past, found herself forgotten at Newport, Rhode Island, where she was slowly but surely falling into disrepair. Franklin Delano Roosevelt resurrected her from this ignominious position and recommissioned her as the flagship of the U.S. Atlantic fleet in 1940, but funds to restore her were lacking, and the ship was towed to Boston. In 1953, a private committee of Baltimore citizens collected sufficient funds to get the ship home to Baltimore and restore her to her pristine glory. This has only just been done, and anyone visiting the *Constellation* at her Baltimore pier makes a small contribution to the maintenance of the old ship. Visitors are admitted,

although no one is permitted to sleep aboard. Ever since I published the account of the ghostly happenings aboard the ship, people, out of curiosity, wanted to spend the night aboard. Since the ship is all wood, fire hazards exist, and the committee cannot permit anyone to stay on after dark. Frankly, I wouldn't if I were just a curious person, because two of the three resident ghosts aboard the U.S.F. *Constellation* are certainly still there.

Those interested in the complete details of the hauntings might talk to the curator, Donald Stewart of Baltimore. The first ghost is an old sailor, by the name of Neil Harvey, who keeps appearing to visitors wearing the uniform of bygone days. With the help of medium Sybil Leek I was able to pinpoint more accurately the other two haunting personalities. They are associated with the so-called orlop deck below the main deck, and the area near where the gun emplacements used to be. The two haunting entities were closely associated with each other. One was the ship's captain Thomas Truxtun. The other was a watch who had fallen asleep on duty and in the cruel manner of the times had been condemned to death by the captain. Death was administered to the unfortunate one by his being strapped to a gun and blown to bits. The executed sailor is the other ghost, and Captain Truxtun's own feelings of guilt perhaps caused him to remain aboard.

Sybil Leek also felt the presence of a cabin boy who somehow had come to grief aboard ship, but she described that event as having happened at a later time, around 1822, whereas the events involving Captain Truxtun took place between 1795 and 1802. As for the man blown to bits, the unfortunate sailor's name was Neil Harvey, and he was been seen at various times by visitors to the ship who knew nothing whatsoever about the ghostly traditions attached to it.

A visit to the U.S.F. *Constellation* is a must if you are ever in the area. There is no need for an advance appointment, nor is it necessary to hide one's interest in the ghostly happenings aboard.

32

The Ghostly Maco Light
North Carolina

Not all ghosts or hauntings are tied to buildings. There are haunted crossroads, haunted airports, and even haunted railroad crossings. One of the most famous of all such phenomena still exists at the railroad crossing near Maco, North Carolina, twelve miles west of Wilmington on the Atlantic Coast Line Railroad. Ever since 1867, an itinerant light has been observed by hundreds upon hundreds of people in the area, which could not be explained on natural grounds. Despite attempts by scientists to explain the light as part of swamp gas, reflected automobile headlights, or other natural origins, these so-called explanations have not really answered the question.

In 1964 I made a thorough investigation of the entire phenomenon, and in the course of it interviewed dozens of actual witnesses who had observed the light. There were several among them who had not only seen a light approach along the tracks where no light should be, but had actually, on getting closer, observed that the light was inside an old railroad lantern; and some had even heard the sound of an approaching train close by. The consensus seems to be that a ghostly personality appears at the Maco trestle holding a railroad lantern aloft as if to warn someone or something. This fits in with the tradition that a certain Joe Baldwin was behind the haunting.

Baldwin was a conductor on what was then called the Wilmington, Manchester and Augusta Railroad, and he was riding in the end coach of a train one night in 1867. The coach somehow left the train and Baldwin grabbed a lantern

in an effort to signal a passenger train which was following close behind. Unfortunately, the engineer of the train did not see the signal and a crash was the result. The only one to lose his life in the crash was Joe Baldwin himself; he was decapitated. The signal lantern was later found a distance from the track. There is no question in my mind that the surviving spirit of Joe Baldwin—who, incidentally, is buried in a Roman Catholic cemetery close by the tracks—is still trying to discharge what he considers his solemn duty. Unfortunately he is not aware of the fact that no train is following him any longer.

Those wishing to watch for the ghostly light at Maco,
North Carolina, can do so freely, but must exercise patience.
Also, there are a considerable number of tourists always in
the area, who come for the same reason. Nevertheless, the
percentage of those who have seen the ghostly lights is amaz-
ingly large. Those wishing additional information about the
area should contact the Southeastern North Carolina Beach
Association, Wilmington, North Carolina.

VI
Private
Ghost Houses,
America

33

The Haunted Hollywood Party
California

Arden Boulevard is in a highly respectable and rather attractive section of Hollywood and contains mainly attractive, small houses with gardens behind them. Back in 1963 I was a panelist on a television program and shortly afterwards received a letter from a lady who seemed to be very upset about the ghosts in her house. As soon as I could, I paid her a visit. She seemed calmer now as she explained what had happened in the house.

"My mother bought our home about 38 years ago. It had just been completed when we moved in. Unfortunately, two years later financial reverses forced us to rent the house out to strangers and live elsewhere. There were five different tenants during the nine-year period when we did not live at the house. But during that time my mother received a call from our former next-door neighbors telling her that the people who were living in our house had had a party, as a result of which a terrible fight had occurred and that they could hear furniture being broken and almost had called the police.

"When the last tenants moved out, my mother discovered that it was all too true, furniture had indeed been broken. We moved back in and tried to settle down in what was again our house. There are two bedrooms in back of the house and a small room which we use as a den. These three rooms have French doors and open into a good-sized patio or garden.

"A short time after we had returned to our house, strange things began to happen. I was then about 20 years old. One night when everyone had gone to bed and my sister had gone out, and I was writing a letter in my bedroom, my locked French doors started to rattle and shake as if someone were desperately trying to get in. It happened that we had just painted the patio floor and that the paint was still wet. The next morning I looked outside for any footprints, but there were none. Whoever it was who had rattled our door certainly didn't leave any footprints?

"Next we would hear a light switch being turned now and then when there was no one in the room. During that period I was married and one night, when my husband was outside the house, I was alone. This was around 9:00 P.M., when I suddenly heard someone turning the knob of the door leading from the laundry to the den. I looked and I actually saw the knob being turned by unseen hands!"

"When my husband returned later we looked all over the house but there was no intruder. Every window was bolted, every door was locked."

"Later I divorced my husband and kept company with another man. One night we returned to the house, which was then empty, when we clearly both heard footsteps coming toward the door from inside the house, as if to meet us."

The phenomenon kept continuing, and Helen, her aged mother and her sister all experienced it. Once Helen found herself at an unseen party, clearly hearing a champagne cork popping and liquid being poured right beside her, yet she could see nothing. This experience repeated itself from time to time in six-week intervals. The party apparently took place in what was then her bedroom. Some unseen person kept whistling songs inside the house. Objects on the dressing table would move by their own volition while everyone was in bed at night. In the middle of the night, Helen would hear someone in the kitchen, kettles being handled, cupboards being opened, as if there were someone looking for something—yet when she checked she found there was no one in the kitchen. But the worst came about three years prior to her getting in touch with me.

"One night about three years ago," she explained, "I got up around midnight to go to the bathroom. While I was in the bathroom I heard loudly and clearly a terrible fight going on in the living room. It was a wordless and desperate struggle. How I got the courage to open the door to the living room I'll never know, but I did. It was completely dark.I saw nothing and the fighting stopped the instant I opened the door!''

Hardly had they recovered from this experience when Helen, her mother, and her sister became witnesses to another fight scene right outside their bedrooms on the patio. It sounded as if every stick of their patio furniture was being broken by people who were fighting desperately but wordlessly, and it lasted several minutes. Needless to say when they checked the next morning, none of their furniture had been touched. Everything was in its place and looked as pretty as it had always been.

There is a double garage on the premises and whenever Helen and her family have guests, she and her mother sleep in the garage. Whenever they do so, they are awakened at night by heavy footsteps walking up to the garage door. They never hear anyone walking away from the garage, however. Since the entire property is enclosed by very high fences and a steel gate across the driveway, it is practically impossible for a human intruder to get into the house or patio. One night Helen had dozed off while watching television when she was rudely awakened by a voice enunciating very clearly and saying loudly, "Oh woe, woe, you've got to go, go go!''

But Helen had no intention of giving up the house she loved so much. Instead, she got in touch with me. I came to the house the following April in the company of a medium gifted with photographic mediumship as well as clairvoyance. The medium's name was Maxine Bell, and she had come highly recommended by the American Society for Psychical Research in Los Angeles.

While Mrs. Bell sat in the front living room, I entered the bedroom, which had been the center of most of the activities of the ghost. There I set up my Zeiss camera, and took a number of black and white photographs with time exposure. One of the pictures, when developed under test conditions, clearly shows the figure of a very young girl in a flimsy dress standing near the window of the bedroom.

Since there had been no one in the room but me, and as the camera was in perfect condition and the development and printing had been done by a laboratory, there was no reason to suspect any foul play. What I came to call the "Ghost in a Negligee" turned out to be the surviving spirit of a very young girl who had apparently fallen victim to that terrible fight Helen and her family kept hearing in the dark.

It appeared that a young girl's body might still be buried in the garden and that her appearance and the subsequent disturbances were connected with it. But no matter how I pleaded with Helen to have the garden dug up to look for the body, if in fact there was a body there, Helen refused out of fear that the neighbors might have strange ideas about it. I haven't heard much from Helen lately and so I am not sure whether the young spirit is still about or whether the wild party is still going on night after night in Helen's bedroom.

34

The Stamford Hills Ghosts
Connecticut

The 1780 House, so named because of the large date 1780 over the door, just beneath the American eagle, is one of the finer Colonial houses in the Stamford, Connecticut area. At the time of this story it was owned and lived in by Mr. and Mrs. Robert Cowan, an advertising executive who has an open mind about such things as ghosts. The house has three levels and the Cowans used for their dining room the large room next to the kitchen in what today might be called ground level or even the cellar.

On the next level were a living room and a kind of sitting room. Beyond that there was a corridor leading to the master bedroom and the den. Upstairs there were two guest rooms and a small attic accessible only through a hole in the ceiling. The house had been built during the American Revolution, standing on a wooded slope and was originally called the Woodpecker Ridge Farm, Stamford, Connecticut. The Cowans later moved to New York City and are presently living in Atlanta, Georgia. They did not sell the house because of the ghosts in it, but because they wanted to be more in the center of a large city.

As soon as we had settled ourselves in front of one of the comfortable fireplaces I asked Mr. Cowan to recount his experiences in the old house. At the time they had been in the house nearly ten years.

"From time to time (once a week or so) during most of the time we've lived here I have noticed unidentifiable movements out of the corner of my eye . . . day or night. Most often, I've noticed this while sitting in our parlor and what I see moving seems to be in the living room. At other times, and only late at night when I am the only one awake, I hear beautiful but unidentified music seemingly played by a full orchestra, as though a radio were on in another part of the house.

"The only place I recall hearing this is in an upstairs bedroom and just after I'd gone to bed. Once I actually got up, opened the bedroom door to ascertain if it was perhaps music from a radio accidently left on, but it wasn't.

"Finally, quite often I've heard a variety of knocks and crashes that do not have any logical source within the structural setup of the house. A very loud smash occurred two weeks ago. You'd have thought a door had fallen off its hinges upstairs, but, as usual, there was nothing out of order.

"My wife, Dorothy, had two very vivid experiences about five years ago. One was in the kitchen, or rather outside of a kitchen window. She was standing at the sink in the evening and happened to glance out the window when she saw a face glaring in at her. It was a dark face, perhaps Indian; it was very hateful and fierce.

"At first she thought it was a distorted reflection in the glass but on looking closer, it was a face glaring directly at her. All she could make out was a face only and as she recalls it, *it seemed translucent*. It didn't disappear, *she did!*

"On a summer afternoon my wife was taking a nap in a back bedroom and was between being awake and being asleep when she heard the sounds of men's voices and the sound of working on the grounds—rakes, and garden tools—right outside of the window. She tried to arouse herself to see who they could be, but she couldn't get up."

As the quietness of the countryside slowly settled over us, I could indeed distinguish faraway, indistinct musical sounds, as if someone were playing a radio at a great distance away. A check revealed no nearby house or parked car whose radio could be responsible for this.

After a while we got up and looked about the room itself. We were standing about quietly admiring the furniture, when both my wife, Catherine and I, and of course the

Cowans, clearly heard footsteps overhead. We decided to assemble upstairs in the smaller room next to the one in which I had heard the steps. The reason was that Mrs. Cowan had experienced a most unusual phenomenon in that particular room.

"It was like lightning," she said, "a bright light suddenly come and gone."

I looked the room over carefully. The windows were arranged in such a manner that a reflection from passing cars was out of the question. Both windows, far apart and on different walls, opened into the dark countryside away from the only road.

Catherine and I sat down on the couch, and the Cowans took chairs. We sat quietly for perhaps 20 minutes, without lights except for a small amount of light filtering in from the stairwell. It was very dark, certainly dark enough for sleep and there was not light enough to write by.

As I was gazing toward the back wall of the little room and wondering about the footsteps I had just heard so clearly, I saw a blinding flash of light, white light, in the corner facing me. It came on and disappeared very quickly, so quickly in fact that my wife, whose head had been turned in another direction at the moment, missed it. But Dorothy Cowan saw it and exclaimed, "There it is again. Exactly as I saw it."

Despite its brevity I was able to observe that the light cast a shadow on the opposite wall, so it could not very well have been an hallucination.

I decided it would be best to bring Ethel Johnson Meyers to the house, and we went back to New York soon after.

Actually two visits with Mrs. Meyers were necessary to clarify the situation. The story was this: a young girl by the name of Lucy, born in 1756, had been in love with a young man named Benjamin. Her grandfather Samuel had killed Benjamin by throwing him down a well in back of the house in 1774. The name Harmon was mentioned. The young man allegedly was buried on the hill and the grandfather was buried to the west of a white structure on the same grounds. The tombstone was broken off at the top. This, according to the medium, was done by vandals.

The fascinating part of all this is that the Stamford, Connecticut, Historical Society and some of their volunteer student helpers were given permission to dig around the historical house and grounds not much later. Picture everyone's surprise when they came up with a tombstone with the name Samuel on it, broken off at the top!

35

The Haunted Basement
Georgia

Mary lives in Atlanta, Georgia. She's a quiet woman who speaks with a charming southern accent and is rather conservative in her way of life. Even her special talent of being able to read the tarot cards for her friends used to be an embarrassment to her because of her religion and because of what the neighbors might say if they found out, not to mention the fact that everyone would want a reading from her.

At the time I met her she had two lovely daughters, Katie, a 15-year-old, and Boots, who was attending college. On the day of Halloween, 1962, she and her girls had moved into an attractive 18-year-old house in Atlanta. It stood in a quiet suburban neighborhood amid other small homes of no particular distinction. Not far from the house are the tracks of a railroad which is nowadays used only for freight. Famous old Fort McPherson is not far away; during the Civil War one of the bloodiest engagements was fought on this spot.

The house has two levels; at street level, there's a large living room which one enters from the front side of the house, then there are three bedrooms and on the right side of the house, a den leading into a kitchen. From one of the bedrooms a stair secured by an iron railing leads into the basement. There is a closet underneath the stairs. In back of the house there is a large patio and there are also outside stairs leading again into the basement. Only the right-hand third of the basement area is actually used by the family; a laundry room occupies most of the space and a wall seals it off from the undeveloped "dirt" area of the basement.

The house itself is cozy and warm, the furniture is pleasant and functional, and if it weren't for the fact that some unusual events occurred in the house, one might never suspect it of being anything but just another ordinary suburban home.

Soon after they had moved in, Mary and her daughters knew there was something very odd about the house. She would wake up in the middle of the night because she heard someone digging down in the basement. She thought this entirely out of the question, but when the noise persisted night after night, she wondered whether the neighbors might be putting in a water pipe. After a while, she decided to find out who was doing the digging. She left her bed and went downstairs, but there was nothing to be seen. There were no rats or mice which could have caused the strange noise. There was no freshly turned-up dirt either. The neighbors weren't doing any digging. Even more mysterious, Mary and her two daughters kept hearing the noise of someone trying to break into the house, always at 2:00 in the morning. And when they checked there was never anyone there. They called the police but the police failed to turn up any clues. Mary installed heavy bolts inside the front and rear doors but the day she returned from an errand to an empty house she found the heavy bolts ripped a\ ay by unseen hands.

At that time Mary was estranged from her doctor husband, and she was afraid to discuss the strange phenomena with him, since he put no stock into psychic phenomena and might have taken advantage of the information to have Mary declared in need of psychiatric treatment. Mary was in the habit of taking afternoon naps but now her naps kept being disturbed by an unseen person entering the house, walking through it as if he or she knew it well, and sometimes even running the water or flushing the toilet! Often, when she was doing her laundry in the basement she would clearly hear footsteps overhead then the sound of drawers being opened and shut and water being run. But when she checked, there was no one about and nothing had changed.

At first she kept the disturbing news from her daughters but soon she discovered that the children had also heard the strange noises. In addition, Katie had felt a pair of hands on her during the night when she knew she was alone in her room. Even in plain daylight such heavy objects as books began to disappear and reappear in other places as if someone were trying to play a game with them.

When Boots came back from school she had no idea what her sister and mother had been through, so it was a shock for her to hear someone using a typewriter in the basement when they all knew that there was no one there and no typewriter in the house. The family held a conference and it was decided that what they had in the house was a ghost, or perhaps several. By now they had gotten used to the idea, however, and it did not frighten them as much as before.

One night Katie was asleep when she awoke with the feeling that she was not alone. As she opened her eyes she saw standing by her bedisde a shadowy figure. Since her mother was in the other bedroom, she knew that it could not have been her.

Soon, Mary and her girls realized that they weren't dealing with just one ghost. On several occasions the quick footsteps of a child were also heard along with the heavier footsteps of an adult. Then someone seemed to be calling out to them by name. One day in January of 1968 when they had gotten accustomed to their unseen visitors, Mary awoke to the sound of music coming from the kitchen area. She investigated this at once but found neither a radio nor any other reason for the music that could be accepted on a rational basis.

She returned to bed and tried to ignore the sounds. Just then two scts of footfalls reached her ears right through the covers. One set of feet seemed to turn toward her daughter Katie's room, while the other pair of feet came right toward her bed, where they stopped. Something ice-cold then seemed to touch her. She screamed in fear and jumped from her bed and this apparently broke the phenomenon and again there was no one about.

Mary began to wonder who the person was in the household who made the phenomenon possible, because she knew enough about psychic phenomena to realize that someone had to be the medium. One night she received the answer. She awakened to the sound of a voice coming from her daughter Katie's room.

A female voice was saying a phrase over and over and Katie was answering by repeating it. She could clearly hear, "golden sand" spoken in a sweet, kindly voice and her daughter Katie repeating it in a childish voice totally different from her normal adult tone. Then she heard Katie clap her hands and say, "Now what can I do?" When Mary entered Katie's room she saw her daughter fast asleep. When questioned the next day about the incident, Katie remembered absolutely nothing.

But the incidents continued. One day Katie saw a woman in her 40s, and felt someone fondling her hair. It seemed a kind gesture and Katie was not afraid. By now Mary wondered whether she herself might not be the person to whom the phenomena occurred rather than just her daughter. She had always had psychic ability so she decided to test this potential mediumship within her. Relaxing deeply in an effort to find out who the ghost was and what the ghost wanted in the house, Mary was able to hear with her inner voice the psychic message sent out from the woman. Over and over again she heard the phrase spoken within her—"I need your help to cross the stream!"

Several days later she heard the same female voice whisper in her ear, "I need your help!" "Where are you?" Mary said aloud. "In the basement, in the dirt." the voice answered. Soon Mary realized there was another ghost in the house, this one male. Mary woke from an afternoon nap because she heard someone come through the front door. She sat up and yelled at the unseen presence to go away and leave her alone. But a man's gruff voice answered her. "She can see me!" But Mary did not see anyone. Still, she became more and more convinced that the man was angry at her for having paid attention to the female ghost and Mary wondered whether the two of them were connected.

Mary called on sincere friends to form a "psychic rescue circle," that is, to try to make contact with the restless ghosts and, if possible, send them away. It didn't help. Soon after, Mary heard the pleading voice again, "I need you. Come to the basement." Mary then went to the basement where she said a prayer for the departed. Whether the prayer did it, or whether the ghosts had finally realized that they were staying on in a house that belonged to another time, there were no further disturbances after that.

36

The Indian Girl Ghost
of Kentucky

Mrs. D. and her son Bucky lived in a comfortable house on a hilltop in suburban Kentucky, not far from Cincinnati, Ohio. It is a pleasant white house, not much different from other houses in the area. The surroundings are lovely and peaceful, and there's a little man-made pond right in front of the house. Nothing about the house or the area looks in the least bit ghostly or unusual. Nevertheless, Mrs. D. needed my help in a very vexing situation.

Six months after Mrs. D. had moved into the house, she began to hear footsteps upstairs, when there was no one about, and the sound of a marble being rolled across the hall. Anything supernatural was totally alien to Mrs. D.

Nevertheless, she has a questioning and alert mind, and was not about to accept these phenomena without finding out what caused them. When the manifestations persisted, she walked up to the foot of the stairs and yelled, "Why don't you just come out and show yourself or say something instead of making all those noises?"

As if in answer, an upstairs door slammed shut and then there was utter silence. After a moment's hesitation, Mrs. D. dashed upstairs and made a complete search. There was no one about and the marble, which seemingly had rolled across the floor, was nowhere to be seen.

When the second Christmas in the new house rolled around, the D.'s were expecting Bucky home from the army. He was going to bring his sergeant and the sergeant's wife with him, since they had become very friendly. They celebrated New Year's Eve in style and high spirits (not the ethereal kind, but the bottled type).

Nevertheless, they were far from inebriated when the sergeant suggested that New Year's Eve was a particularly suitable night for a séance. Mrs. D. would have no part of it at first. She had read all about phony séances and remembered what her Bible said about such matters. But later, after her husband had gone to bed, the four of them decided to have a go at it.

They joined hands and sat quietly in front of the fireplace. Nothing much happened for a while. Then Bucky, who had read some books on psychic phenomena, suggested that they needed a guide or control from the other side of life to help them, but no one had any suggestions concerning to whom they might turn.

More in jest than as a serious proposal, Mrs. D. heard herself say, "Why don't you call your Indian ancestor, Little White Flower!" Mr. D. is part Cherokee, and Bucky, the son, would, of course, consider this part of his inheritance too. Mrs. D. protested that all this was nonsense, and they should go to bed. She assured them that nothing was likely to happen. But the other three were too busy to reply, staring behind her into the fireplace. When she followed the direction of their eyes she saw what appeared to be some kind of light similar to that made by a flashlight. It stayed on for a short time and then disappeared altogether.

From that day on, Mrs. D. started to find strange objects around the house that had not been there a moment before. They were little stones in the shape of Indian arrows. She threw them out as fast as she found them. Several weeks later, when she was changing the sheets on her bed, she noticed a huge red arrow had been painted on the bottom sheet—by unseen hands.

One afternoon she was lying down on the couch with a book trying to rest. Before long she was asleep. Suddenly she awoke with a feeling of horror which seemed to start at her feet and gradually work its way up throughout her entire body and mind. The room seemed to be permeated with something terribly evil. She could neither see nor hear anything, but she had the feeling that there was a presence there and that it was very strong and about to overcome her.

For a few weeks she felt quite alone in the house, but then things started up again. The little stone arrowheads appeared out of nowhere again, all over the house. Hysterical with fear, Mrs. D. called upon a friend who had dabbled in metaphysics and asked for advice. The friend advised a séance in order to ask Little White Flower to leave.

Although Little White Flower was not in evidence continually and seemed to come and go, Mrs. D. felt the Indian woman's influence upon her at all times. Later the same week, Little White Flower put in another appearance, this time visual. It was toward four o'clock in the morning, when Mrs. D. woke up with the firm impression that her tormentor was in the room. As she looked out into the hall, she saw on the wall a little red object resembling a human eye, and directly below it what seemed like half a mouth. Looking closer, she discerned two red eyes and a white mouth below. It reminded her of some clowns she had seen in the circus. The vision remained on the wall for two or three minutes, and then vanished completely.

After several postponements, I was finally able to come to Kentucky and meet with Mrs. D. in person. On June 20, 1964, I sat opposite the slightly portly, middle-aged lady who had corresponded with me so voluminously for several months.

As I intoned my solemn exorcism and demanded Little White Flower's withdrawal from the spot, I could hear Mrs. D. crying hysterically. It was almost as if some part of her was being torn out and for a while it seemed that *she* was being sent away, not Little White Flower.

The house has been quiet ever since; Little White Flower has presumably gone back to her own people and Mrs. D. continues living in the house without further disturbances.

37

The Haunted Trailer
Massachusetts

Outside Boston in Peabody, Massachusetts, in a trailer park, lives a lovely lady of Austrian descent by the name of Rita Atlanta. That is not her real name, to be sure, but the name under which she dances in nightclubs. Rita came to America at an early age after undergoing some horrifying experiences at the hands of occupying Russian troops in her native Austria.

She became a well-known dancer in nightclubs both in this country and in Europe and it was in Frankfurt, Germany where we first met. At that time she had read one of my books and had explained to me that she needed some advice concerning a ghostly apparition in her trailer. It seems unusual to hear about ghosts in so modern a residence as a trailer camp but I have heard of ghosts in airplanes and in modern apartment buildings, so I was not particularly surprised.

We spent about an hour talking about Miss Atlanta's other ESP incidents, of which she had a number over the years, and looked at her album of show business photographs. Whenever Rita did not travel on business, she and her teenage son lived in a trailer outside Boston. Sometimes they spent months at a time there when things were slow in the nightclub business.

The boy went to school nearby, being looked after by the grandmother. The trailer itself is fairly large and looks no different from any other trailers of this type, that is to say trailers that are not likely to travel anywhere but are put on a firm base in a camp and are expected to remain there. The

sides are made of metal and inside the trailer there are a large bedroom, a dining room, a kitchen and a small room, almost the same as if this were a conventional small apartment. To be sure, space is tight, but it seemed a comfortable home to me when I visited it a little later.

The reason Miss Atlanta was upset by the goings-on in her trailer had to do with something that happened night after night, at 3:00 in the morning. She would wake from deep sleep to see a man, wearing a dark overcoat, standing in front of her bed and staring at her. She could not make out his face nor could she see his feet, yet there was no mistaking the tall figure of a man coming out of nowhere without the benefit of doors opening, and clearly for reasons of his own.

It did not frighten Rita, for she had had psychic experiences before. But she began to wonder why this stranger kept appearing to her in what she knew was a new trailer, having bought it herself a few years prior. Even her son saw the stranger on one occasion. So she knew that it was not her active imagination causing her to see things.

She began to ask questions of neighbors, people living in other trailers in the camp. Finally, she came upon an assistant to the manager of the camp who had been there for a long time. He nodded seriously when she described what was occurring in her trailer. Then he showed her a spot on the road just in front of it, explaining that it was there where she would find the cause of her problem. Some years before a man roughly fitting the description she had given had been run over and killed by a car. Clearly then, Rita Atlanta figured, the apparition she had seen in her trailer was that of the restless spirit of the man who had died in front of it and was confused as to his true status. Whenever his spirit recalled the moment of his untimely death, he apparently had felt a compulsion to look for help and the nearest place to look would have been her trailer.

Ever since Rita and I discussed this over coffee in her trailer, the apparition has not returned.

38

The Phantom Admiral
New Hampshire

The Jacobsen family has a lovely summer home in their town in New Hampshire. The house stands in a secluded part of the forest at the end of a narrow winding driveway lined by tall trees, and there is a wooden porch around it on three sides. The house itself rises up three stories and is painted white in the usual New England manner.

The house was called "Mish' Top" by its original owner and builder, an admiral. I questioned Erlend Jacobsen, who was on the Goddard College faculty as an instructor, about his experiences in the old house.

"When my parents decided to turn the attic into a club room where I could play with my friends," Erlend Jacobsen began, "they cut windows into the wall and threw out all the possessions of the former owner of the house that they found there. I was about seven at the time.

"Soon after, footsteps and other noises began to be heard in the attic and along the corridors and stairs leading toward it. But it wasn't until the summer of 1955 that I experienced my first really important disturbance. That summer we slept here for the first time in this room, one flight up, and almost nightly we were either awakened by noises or could not sleep, waiting for them to begin. At first we thought they were animal noises, but they were too much like footsteps and heavy objects being moved across the floor overhead, and down the hall. We were so scared we refused to move in our beds or turn down the lights."

"But you did know of the tradition that the house was haunted, did you not?" I asked.

"Yes, I grew up with it. All I knew is what I had heard from my parents. The original owner and builder of the house, an admiral named Hawley, and his wife, were both most difficult people. The admiral died in 1933. In 1935 the house was sold to my parents by his daughter, who was then living in Washington. Anyone who happened to be trespassing on his territory would be chased off it, and I imagine he would not have liked our throwing out his sea chest and other personal possessions."

"Any other experience outside the footsteps?"

"About four years ago," Erlend Jacobsen replied, "my wife and I, and a neighbor, Sheppard Vogelsang, were sitting in the living room downstairs discussing interpretations of the Bible. I needed a dictionary at one point in the discussion and got up to fetch it from upstairs.

"I ran up to the bend here, in front of this room, and there were no lights on at the time. I opened the door to the clubroom and started to go up the stairs, when suddenly I walked into what I can only describe as a *warm, wet blanket*, something that touched me physically as if it had been hung from wires in the corridor. I was very upset, backed out and went downstairs. My wife took one look at me and said, 'you're white.' 'I know,' I said. 'I think I just walked into the admiral.' "

"Has anyone else had an encounter with a ghost here?" I asked.

"Well another house guest went up into the attic and came running down reporting that the door knob had turned in front of his very eyes before he coud reach for it to open the door. The dog was with him, and steadfastly refused to cross the threshold. Another house guest arrived very late at night, about five years ago. We had already gone to bed, and he knew he had to sleep in the attic since every other room was already taken. Instead, I found him sleeping in the living room, on the floor, in the morning. He knew nothing about the ghost. 'I'm not going back up there any more,' he vowed, and would not say anything further. I guess he must have run into the admiral."

Every member of the family had at one time or another had an encounter with the ghostly admiral, it appeared. Sybil Leek, my mediumistic friend, had come with us and soon she was able to pick up the vibrations of the unseen visitor. As soon as she had gone into a trance state she made contact with the admiral. She even had the name right, although she had not been present when I had spoken to the owners of the house earlier!

It seemed that the admiral had resented the new owners' throwing out all of his things. He did not like the house having been sold the way it was, but would have preferred it to go to his son. I implored the ghostly admiral not to upset the family now living in the house and he replied, in rather a stiff navy manner, that he was a tidy person and would take care of himself. When we left, it seems to me that the old sea dog must have felt a lot better; after all, how many New Yorkers would drive all the way up to New Hampshire to talk to him after all those years?

39

The Little Old Lady Ghost
Of Bank Street
New York City

What I'm about to relate happened in 1957, but the house is still there, and perhaps even the owners haven't changed. It was then a private house in New York City, and in the heart of Greenwich Village on Bank Street. There are many ancient houses on Bank Street, but this one is special: the ghost who 'lived' there was not ancient at all—far from it.

At the time when I became involved with it, or rather with the ghost in it, it belonged to Dr. Harvey Slatin, an engineer by profession, and his wife, the artist Yeffe Kimball, who is an Osage Indian. The house in which they lived was then 125 years old, made of red brick, and still in excellent condition.

Digging into the past of their home, the Slatins established that a Mrs. Maccario had run the house as a 19-room boarding establishment for years, before selling it to them. However, Mrs. Maccario wasn't of much help when questioned. She knew nothing of her predecessors.

After the Slatins had acquired the house, and the other tenants had finally left, they did the house over. The downstairs became one long living room, extending from front to back, adorned with a fireplace and a number of good paintings and ceramics. In the back part of this room, the Slatins placed a heavy wooden table. The rear door led to a small garden, and a narrow staircase led to the second floor.

During quiet moments, they often thought they heard a woman's footsteps on the staircase, sometimes crossing the upper floors, sometimes a sound like a light hammering.

Strangely enough, the sounds were heard more often in the daytime than at night, a habit most unbecoming a traditional haunt. The Slatins were never frightened by this. They simply went to investigate what might have caused the noises, but never found any visible evidence. There was no "rational" explanation for them, either.

One Sunday in January of 1957, they decided to clock the noises, and found that the ghostly goings-on lasted all day; during these hours, they would run upstairs to trap the trespasser—only to find empty rooms and corridors. Calling out to the Unseen brought no reply, either. An English carpenter by the name of Arthur Brodie was as well-adjusted to reality as are the Slatins, but he also heard the footsteps. His explanation that "one hears all sorts of noises in old houses" did not help matters any. Sadie, the maid, heard the noises too, and after an initial period of panic, got accustomed to them as if they were part of the house's routine—which indeed they were!

One morning in February, Arthur Brodie was working in a room on the top floor, hammering away at the ceiling. He was standing on a stepladder that allowed him to just about touch the ceiling. Suddenly, plaster and dust showered down on his head, and something heavy fell and hit the floor below. Mrs. Slatin in her first-floor bedroom heard the thump. Before she could investigate the source of the loud noise, there was Brodie at her door, saying: "It's me, Ma'am, Brodie. I'm leaving the job! I've found the body!" But he was being facetious. What he actually found was a black-painted metal container about twice the size of a coffee can. On it there was a partially faded label, reading *"The last remains of Elizabeth Bullock, deceased. Cremated January 21, 1931."* The label also bore the imprint of the United States Crematory Company, Ltd., Middle Village, Borough of Queens, New York, and stamped on the top of the can was the number—37251.

Curiously, the ceiling that had hidden the container dated back at least to 1880, which was long before Elizabeth Bullock had died. One day, the frail woman crossed Hudson

Street, a few blocks from the Slatin residence. A motorist going at full speed saw her too late, and she was run over. Helpful hands carried her to a nearby drugstore, while other bystanders called for an ambulance. But help arrived too late for Mrs. Bullock. She died at the drugstore before any medical help arrived. Strangely enough, when Dr. Slatin looked through the records, he found that Mrs. Bullock had never lived in this street at all!

Still, Mrs. Bullock's ashes were found in that house. How to explain that? In the crematory's books, her home address was listed at 113 Perry Street. Dr. Slatin called on Charles Dominick, the undertaker in the case. His place of business had been on West 11th Street, not far from Bank Street.

Upon invitation by the owners of the house I arranged for a séance with the help of medium Ethel Johnson Meyers and on July 17, 1957, we tried to make contact with the restless spirit of Mrs. Bullock. We then realized why Mrs. Bullock could not find peace and didn't mind hanging around the house on Bank Street for the time being, where, after all, her ashes were being kept. She married out of the faith, she explained to the medium, and in those days that was a serious breach of family tradition.

It was her husband who had stolen the ashes and hidden them in a nearby house, and when repairs were made in that house the canister was stowed away where no one was likely to find it. But what now? I asked the ghost. What would she like us to do with the ashes? The ghost was adamant about being buried with her own family. Her mother would not forgive her for having married a man outside the Roman Catholic faith. But being buried in a Presbyterian cemetary, to please her late husband, would not do either, because it might upset her family. "Then what?" I demand to know. But the solution came from the owners of the house, not from the ghost. A simple grave was arranged for the late Mrs. Bullock in the backyard, with an equally simple non-denomination cross above it. And there the ghost, and the story, rest.

40

June Havoc's Haunted Town House
New York City

On West 44th Street, in Manhattan, stands an impressive town house built more than a hundred years ago. Originally the property of the Rodenberg family, the four-story stone house passed into the possession of a certain man named Payne. Using the original building plans to restore the Victorian house, he made no changes in the structure and tried to follow all the plans when he restored the house to its original form in the 1950s. Between 1962 and 1969 the building was the property of the well-known stage and screen actress, June Havoc. She rented the upper floors to various tenants, but she used the downstairs appartment for herself.

Miss Havoc's former apartment is reached by a staircase to the parlor floor. For some strange reason, tenants never stayed very long in that ground-floor apartment, but Miss Havoc paid no special attention at the time. Before long, however, she noticed a number of strange things. Tapping noises at various times of day and night kept her from sleeping or concentrating on her work. They were not the kind of noises one could explain away by natural causes. Miss Havoc made sure of that by having experts come to the house and examine steampipes, flooring, and walls. The main area of activity seemed to be the kitchen and the rear section of the house.

I held two séances at the house with medium Sybil Leek. On the first occasion, an entity calling herself Lucy Ryan made a noisy entrance by demanding something to eat in a loud voice not at all like Sybil's own.

I immediately questioned the spirit and discovered that she had starved to death during a fever epidemic. She claimed to have lived in the year 1792. Also, a fever epidemic had occurred at that time and Colonel Napier himself had been shipped back to England in very poor condition.

We freed Lucy from that house and vice versa. In a second séance we tried to get rid of the soldier. Unfortunately, he was of sterner stuff. Complaints of noisy phenomena keep coming to me, so I must assume dear Alfred has not quite left.

Miss Havoc has since sold the house, ghost and all. How the current owners feel about visitors I can only guess.

41

The Case of the Tipsy Ghost
New York City

The Quick and the Dead aren't always as different as you might think. Take, for instance, the case of the Restless Advertising Executive who insisted on his usual Martini even after he had committed suicide.

It all started when my friend and fellow ghost devotee, the late *New York Daily News* columnist Danton Walker, ran the following tantalizing item:

> West 56th Street agitated by what purports to be the ghost of a former Madison Avenue ad executive who was ruined by drink. Makes his pre-dawn presence known by scribbling advertising slogans on the building walls and leaving an empty Martini glass on the bar of his former restaurant hangout.

It didn't take me long to track down the restaurant, which turned out to be a posh eatery known as DaVinci's. I arranged with the owner to hold a séance in the place, and to find out what it was that disturbed our drinking ghost.

The DaVinci owners were very co-operative. After all, why not? If the place is so good that even the dead want to return there for a visit, the living ought to be lining up, too. And apparently this was not the clanking variety of ghost, but a jolly fellow with a keen sense of humor.

I telephoned Ethel Meyers. She agreed to come along, although I told her nothing of our destination. We met late at night, after the usual dinner guests and even the late-hour tipplers had gone, and the DaVinci was practically empty. The last persistent barflies I chased myself by telling them the place was haunted. Rather than wait to find out if it really was, they departed in great haste.

Present in the longish room there remained the late Broadway director Harold Clurman, with his silver cane and imperturbable mien, who really didn't care at all for ghosts; and his fiancée and later wife, actress Juleen Compton, who very much cared, especially since she had seen the ghost of the advertising man in what had once been his apartment and had since become hers. There he was, she related, here one moment, gone the next.

That's how ghosts are, I assured her.

Alas, she knew him well—when among the Quick —and felt that any help she could give him now, she would gladly give. The man deserved a rest, after all. Apparently he had committed suicide while not entirely sober, and that is frequently the cause of a haunting—when the ghost wakes up dead, so to speak, and doesn't like it!

The lights were doused, and we seated ourselves behind the long table on one side of the room. I was next to Mrs. Meyers. Within minutes, she was in deep trance, completely oblivious to what went on around her. In this state of total dissociation, the psychic lends her vocal apparatus and body to a discarnate entity, and it is his or her personality that speaks through the facilities of the medium. This is easy to check: if the information obtained in this manner is unknown to all present, especially to the psychic, and is of a personal nature rather than general and obtainable without too much trouble, then we have a genuine communication.

No sooner was Mrs. Meyers in deep trance, than our friend took over. In a creaking voice very unlike Mrs. Meyers' own soft-spoken tones, he demanded a drink—*any drink*—refusing to talk about anything until his drink had been brought. We went through the motions of putting a glass into the medium's hands, but evidently the ghost was also using her smelling faculties, for he immediately bellowed that the glass was empty!

With that, he began to rock the table rather violently, all the time insisting on his drink. Remember, Mrs. Meyers was not told that the ghost had been an alcholic or that this was his favorite place. We finally put a Martini before Mrs.

Meyers (who doesn't drink herself and would have been horrified at the sight). Our ghost calmed down somewhat, enough for me to ask some questions. When I brought up the fact that he had killed himself, he started to cry for "Allan, Allan," and I quickly looked at Miss Compton's face to see if it meant anything. It did. Later, she told me that the ghost had spent his last day on earth drinking with Allan, his closest friend.

As is usual in these investigations, once contact is made, I tell the Restless One that he should leave and go to what Dr. Joseph Rhine of Duke Univeristy calls the "World of the Mind," that wider horizon where human memory continues to live beyond the confines of space and time, and, certainly, of the physical body.

Then I proceeded to awaken Mrs. Meyers from her "alcoholic" trance, while the Da Vinci waiters and staff stood transfixed behind the rear door, watching in awe.

"Where am I? Hic!" my psychic lady said, and looked properly amazed.

It was the first time in my long career as a Ghost Hunter that anyone had become inebriated by a ghost. But the fact was, Mrs. Meyers had a king-size hangover.

42

Lucy and Her Virginia House Ghosts

A quiet Virginia community, not far from Washington, D.C., boasts a number of lovely old houses, among them on belonging to Mrs. Lucy Dickey at the time when I visited it.

When we arrived at the Dickey House, I was immediately impressed by the comparative grandeur of its appearance. Although not a very large house, it nevertheless gave the impression of a country manor—the way it was set back from the road amid the trees, with a view toward a somewhat wild garden in the rear. A few steps led up to the front entrance. We entered a large living room that led to a passage into a dining room and thence into the kitchen. In the center of the ground floor is a staircase to another floor, and from the second floor, on which most of the bedrooms are located, there is a narrow staircase to a garret that contains another bedroom.

The house was beautifully furnished in late Colonial style, and antiques had been set out in the proper places with a display of taste not always met these days.

"What made you think there was something unusual about the house after you moved in?" I asked Mrs. Dickey.

"I was about the last member of the family to be aware that something was going on, but I had heard repeated stories from the children. I was sleeping in one of the children's rooms upstairs one night, and was awakened by heavy footsteps—not in the room but in the next room. I wondered who was up, and, I heard them walking back and forth and back and forth. I finally went back to sleep, but I was kind of excited. The next morning I asked who was up during the night, and no one had been up.''

"What was the next thing?"

"I was sleeping in my son Douglas' room again, and I was having a very frightening dream. I don't remember what the dream was, but I was terrified. Suddenly I awoke and looked at the wall. Before I had gone off to sleep, I had noticed that the room had been sort of flooded with panels of light, and there were two shafts of light side by side, right directly at the wall. I sat right up in bed and I looked up and there was the *shadow of a head*. I don't know whether it was a man's or a woman's, because there were no features, but there was a neck, there was hair, it was the size of a head, and it was high up on the wall. It could have been a woman with short, bushy hair. It was so real that I thought it was Joyce, my daughter, who was about 18 then. I said, 'Joyce,' and I started speaking to it. Then I realized it was waving a little bit. I became frightened. After about ten minutes of my saying, 'Joyce, Joyce, who is it? Who is there?', it moved directly sideways, into the darkness and into the next panel of light, and by then I was crying out, 'Joyce, Joyce, where are you?' I wanted someone to see it with me.''

"What was the next event that happened after that?"

"In 1967 we decided to get a Ouija board. We had some friends who knew this house well, and said, 'You ought to work a board and find out what was there.' They owned this house for about ten or fifteen years; their names are Dean and Jean Vanderhoff.

"On several occasions they heard a woman talking in the kitchen when there was no other woman in the house. They heard the voice, and they also heard the heavy garage doors bang up and down at night, with great noise.''

"What did you decide to do after that?" Apparently, the Dickey family decided to use the time-honored Ouija board to find out who was causing all the problems. Immediately they received the names of two people, Martha and Morgan.

"Martha said that it was *she* who was appearing on the wall, because one child in the next room had fallen out of bed, and Martha loves children, and tried to help. And Martha said dear things about me—that I have a big job, and it's hard for me to handle the children, and she's here to help."

"Does she give you any evidence of her existence as a person?"

"I think she and Morgan are brother and sister and they're both children of Sarah. And Sarah was the first wife of Homer Leroy Salisbury who built this house in 1865."

Apparently a lot of the phenomena started when structural changes were made in the house, altering its appearance from what it was in the nineteenth century. Even people, not members of the family, who stay at the house soon come face-to-face with the ghost or at least one of them.

"A friend, Pat Hughes, saw a woman here one night. Pat was here with a man named Jackson McBride, and they were talking, and at three o'clock I left and went to bed. At about four o'clock in the morning, Pat heard noises in the kitchen and thought I had gotten up. She heard someone walking back and forth. Pat was over there, and said, 'Come on in, Lucy, stop being silly. Come in and talk to us.' And this apparition walked in, and then Pat said, 'It's not Lucy'—she realized that the ghost looked somewhat like me. It was tall and slim, had long dark hair, and had a red robe on and something like a shawl collar, and her hand was holding the collar. Pat was excited and said, 'My God, it's not lucy! *Who is it?*' She said to this man, 'Come and look,' but he was afraid. Then Pat turned to go back and try to communicate, but it had vanished! Later, they heard a great rattle of things in the kitchen."

Several months later I returned to the house in the company of Ethel Johnson Meyers. That's when we met another spirit named Emma, connected with the house. Someone named Leon had apparently killed her. We tried to assure the restless spirits that they need not hang around the house any longer and to go on into the next state of existence. Apparently this worked, for I heard again from Lucy Dickey several months later when she assured me that things in the house had become completely quiet. However, she had decided to sell the house after all, and move to a smaller apartment.

If you happen to be in Vienna, Virginia, and somehow manage to be allowed inside the former Dickey homestead, you are likely to meet up with at least one if not several of the resident ghosts, because I have the feeling that we haven't dispatched them all, if any.

VII
Houses in the British Isles

43

The Nell Gwyn House
London

Anyone familiar with the London nightclub scene has at one time or another been past a rather garish sign advertising the Gargoyle Club. Together with the Nell Gwyn Theatre, this establishment is housed in what at first appears to be a house of nondescript appearance, and on close examination it clearly shows its age. As a matter of fact, the building itself was erected in 1632 as part of the royal saddlery. Located near the Deanery of St. Paul's, it is now at number 69 Dean Street.

One gains entrance to the building from a side street, not from Dean Street itself. An elevator goes up to the third floor. It is a very small and slow elevator, in keeping with the narrowness of the stairwell. In addition to the two theatres, one atop the other, there are dressing rooms, an office, and sundry rooms. Finally, there is an open roof on which one can walk.

The insides are no more tawdry than the interior of other nightclubs of this kind, and though performers do not wear any clothes—or almost none—it is by no means a wide-open house in any sense of the term. Prices are modest by American standards, and the shows are not without merit. Various dancers and strippers have at times heard voices, footsteps, seen doors open by themselves, or been disturbed by the noise of documents being handled in total darkness. Some of them had their names called by unseen presences. Mr. Jacobs, the former owner, now deceased, had actually seen a "gray lady" emerge from the elevator shaft, even though the elevator had not opened its doors, and glide by him only to disappear into the opposite wall.

At one time the ancient Royalty Theatre stood next door to the Gargoyle Club, and Jacobs thought for a long time that the ghost was one of the actresses from the Royalty, next door. During the London blitz, the royalty Theatre was demolished. The phenomena, however, continued.

On two separate occasions I took two celebrated London trançe mediums to the Gargoyle. They were Ronald Hearn and Miss Trixie Allingham. Independently, however, they insisted that the unrestful presence was Nell Gwyn, and in both cases Nell herself came through in full trance to speak to me of her troubles.

It appears that 69 Dean Street had been Nell Gwyn's private apartment, given to her by King Charles II so that he could have her close by rather than riding off to Salisbury Hall, the country place he had purchased for his beloved Nell. Here, close by Whitehall, the Royal Palace, he could visit her more frequently and with less likelihood of being observed. Unfortunately there were times when Nell was all by herself. It did not suit her theatrical temperament to be neglected, even by so illustrious a suitor as the king. Somehow, she struck up an affair with one of the king's officers by the name of Captain John Molyneaux, of the Royal Cavalry. However, the king found out. He sent another one of his officers, a Lieutenant Fortescus, with a group of men to the apartment looking for the captain. At the time of the raid, Nell was in the "salon," and Fortescue engaged the captain in a duel on the stairwell. They fought to the finish up the stairs and onto the roof, where Nell's lover fell mortally wounded.

That in essence was the story obtained by psychic means through the mouths of two entranced mediums.

Nell herself was bound to the place not because of King Charles, but because of the death of her lover on the stairs. Whether she herself is still present, or perhaps only the *impression* of her, is hard to say. At any rate, I was able to trace both officers' names in contemporary records, and there is no doubt that number 69 Dean Street was the place of this ancient tragedy.

44

Hall Place
Kent

Off the main London-Bexley road, in Kent, stands a thirteenth century manor house called Hall Place. During the Tudor period it was largely rebuilt and, therefore, presents more of a Tudor appearance than an early medieval picture. It has three stories and four wings, thus is one of the larger mansions of this type and suitable for its present purpose, a school. By car it can easily be reached in an hour's drive from London. Since it is a school, permission need not necessarily be obtained to enter it, but it is wiser to call the school

director if one wishes to have a personally conducted tour by a member of the staff.

Of course, Hall Place does not advertise its haunting, nor are the present tenants particularly interested in it. It is wisest, therefore, to motivate one's impending visit on historical grounds.

There is a tradition attached to the mansion that Lady Atte-Hall threw herself to her death from one of the towers when she saw her husband killed by a stag. Strange noises and groans have indeed been reported from the area of the tower, and a so-called "white woman" has been seen there. In 1931, Canon Wicksted conducted exorcism ceremonies in the place. Finally, a local psychic research society at Lewisham spent a night at Hall Place, but experienced nothing special.

I brought famed British psychic Douglas Johnson to the Hall without telling him where we were going that afternoon. He felt that someone had hanged himself in the upper part of the building, in what is actually the servants' quarters, and who may have been a servant. Mr. Johnson also psychically saw a woman worried about a child, and that the child had been murdered.

This is one of those places where the visitors must discover their own hauntings. It may well be that there are others of which we have no record as yet. Either way, a visit to Hall Place, Bexley Heath, is definitely worthwhile.

45

The Tower
London

Probably the most celebrated of British royal ghosts is the shade of unlucky Queen Anne Boleyn, the second wife of Henry VIII, who ended her days on the scaffold. Accused of infidelity, which was a form of treason in the sixteenth century, she had her head cut off despite protestations of her innocence. In retrospect, historians have well established that she was speaking the truth. But at the time of her trial, it was a political matter to have her removed from the scene, and even her uncle, who sat in judgment of her as the trial judge, had no inclination to save her neck.

Anne Boleyn's ghost has been reported in a number of places connected with her in her lifetime. There is, first of all, her apparition at Hampton Court, attested to by a number of witnesses over the years, and even at Windsor Castle, where she is reported to have walked along the eastern parapet. At the so-called Salt Tower within the confines of the Tower of London, a guard observed her ghost walking along headless, and he promptly fainted. The case is on record, and the man insisted over and over again that he had not been drinking.

Perhaps he would have received a good deal of sympathy from a certain Lieutenant Glynn, a member of the Royal Guard, who has stated, also for the record, "I have seen the great Queen Elizabeth and recognized her, with her olive skin color, her fire-red hair, and her ugly dark teeth. There is no doubt about it in my mind." Although Elizabeth died a natural death at a ripe old age, it is in the nature of ghosts that both the victims and the perpetrators of crimes sometimes becomes restless once they have left the physical body. In the case of good Queen Bess, there was plenty to be remorseful over. Although most observers assume Queen Elizabeth "walks" because of what she did to Mary Queen of Scots, I disagree. Mary had plotted against Elizabeth, and her execution was legal in terms of the times and conditions under which the events took place. If Queen Elizabeth I has anything to keep her restless, it would have to be found among the many lesser figures who owed their demise to her anger or cold cunning, including several ex-lovers.

Exactly as described in the popular English ballad, Anne Boleyn had been observed with "her 'ead tucked under," not only at the Tower of London, but also at Hever Castle, in Kent, where she was courted by King Henry VIII.

46

**The Garrick's Head Inn
Bath**

Three hours by car from London is the elegant resort city of Bath. Here, in a Regency architectural wonderland, there is an eighteenth century inn called Garrick's Head Inn. At one time there was a connection between the inn and the theatre next door, but the theatre no longer exists. In the eighteenth century, the famous gambler Beau Nash owned this inn which was then a gambling casino as well.

The downstairs bar looks like any other bar, divided as it is between a large, rather dark room where the customers sip their drinks, and a heavy wooden bar behind which the owner dispenses liquor and small talk. There is an upstairs, however, with a window that, tradition says, is impossible to keep closed for some reason. The rooms upstairs are no longer used for guests, but are mainly storage rooms or private rooms of the owners. At the time of my first visit to the Garricks Head Inn it was owned by Bill Loud, who was a firm skeptic when he had arrived in Bath. Within two months, however, his skepticism was shattered by the phenomena he was able to witness. The heavy till once took off by itself and smashed a chair. The noises of people walking were heard at night at a time when the place was entirely empty. He once walked into what he described as "cobwebs" and felt his head stroked by a gentle hand. He also smelled perfume when he was entirely alone in the cellar.

A reporter from a Bristol newspaper, who spent the night at the inn, also vouched for the authenticity of the footsteps and strange noises.

Finally, the owner decided to dig into the past of the building, and he discovered that there have been incidents which could very well be the basis for the haunting. During the ownership of gambling king Beau Nash, there had been an argument one night, and two men had words over a woman. A duel followed. The winner was to take possession of the girl. One man was killed and the survivor rushed up the stairs to claim his prize. The girl, who had started to flee when she saw him win, was not agreeable, and when she heard him coming barricaded herself in the upstairs room and hanged herself.

Whether you will see or hear the lady ghost at the Garrick's Head Inn in Bath is a matter of individual ability to communicate with the psychic world. It also depends upon the hours of the night you go there, for the Garrick's Head Inn is pretty noisy in the early part of the evening when it is filled with people looking for spirits in the bottle rather than the more ethereal kind.

47

The Ghostly Monks at
Beaulieu, Hampshire

Not far from Southampton stands the Abbey of Beaulieu, dating back to the early Middle Ages. It is now mostly a ruin although some parts of it have been restored, especially the Early English refectory or dining hall of the monks, which has been turned into a chapel.

Actually, Beaulieu has two major tourist attractions. One is the old Abbey, the other is Palace House, the residence of the Barons Montague of Beaulieu, built mainly during the fifteenth century and restored later.

Next to the Palace House, the present Lord Montagu has turned his interest in unusual automobiles into a profitable sideline: the Beaulieu Motor Museum is known the world over. Neither Palace House nor museum has any psychic connotations, of course.

As with many British abbeys or monasteries, the dissolution order of Henry VIII was by no means the end of the presence of monks. Sometimes these people had no other place to go, even in death, and their spirits seem to want to hang on to the old masonry with which they were familiar during their lives.

Ghostly monks have been observed by visitors in the ruined abbey itself and along the pathways leading toward it. In the Beaulieu chapel, once the monks' refectory, two lady visitors saw the scene as it was when the monks used it to dine. Others have heard the choir sing in the empty church. Monks reading scrolls on the stones, walking in what was once a garden, digging a grave in the dead of night to bury one of their own—these are some of the things that people have reported during the past few years. It is a fact that the

monks' own burial ground has never been discovered. There is a cemetery for the villagers, but none of the monks are buried there. Could it be that the restless monks are looking for their own burial ground?

To a visitor, Beaulieu offers many attractions, not the least of which is the possibility of running into a man in a brown habit. If he looks like a monk, please remember—there haven't been any monks at Beaulieu for centuries.

To reach Beaulieu by car from London or from Southampton is quite easy. From London; one has to figure an entire day, getting back late at night. En route, one might conceivably stop at Stonehenge, but there are two or three other attractions of psychic interest in the area that one might go to the following day.

No special permission is required to visit the ruined abbey, but there is a fee for visiting Palace House and it is wise to inquire beforehand if someone might be available to guide you into the haunted portions of the Abbey ruins. Address yourself to Lord Montagu's factor, or manager, at Palace House, Beaulieu, Hampshire, England.

48

Longleat Palace
Bath

Across England, in the west, and not far from the city of Bath, stands the huge country house Longleat, ancestral seat of the Marquises of Bath. From a distance this white building looks majestic and very much like a fairy tale palace. There are swans in some of the ponds in the large park for which Longleat was famous.

As with so many large estates, the owners had to "go public" to defray the expense of keeping the place in order and pay taxes. Visitors are not only permitted, they are actively encouraged to come. There are extra attractions, such as a zoo with a large number of lions, and dining facilities on the grounds. The ordinary tourist comes for that and the magnificent art in the house. Very few people think of ghosts when visiting Longleat. However, if you wish to see the so-called haunted areas, it would be wiser to write ahead of time and ask for a special tour. Some of these spots are on the "regular" tourist route for all visitors, some are in the private portion of Longleat.

By 1580 the main portion of the house was already in existence, but it was later added to and finally rebuilt in the seventeen century when it achieved its current appearance. The original owner was a certain Sir John Thynne, a financier to the royal family, who had acquired the property during a period of stress in English history. He and his successors managed to amass a fortune in fine art and fill Longleat with it from ground floor to the roof. The present Lord Bath lives in a considerably more modest place, not far away.

There are three sets of ghosts at Longleat. To begin with, in the so-called red library the apparition of a "scholarly-looking man wearing a high collar and the costume of the sixteenth century" has been seen. He is believed to be the builder of Longleat, Sir John Thynne. He may be kept roaming the corridors for personal reasons connected with the acquisition of the property.

Upstairs there is a haunted corridor with a long, narrow passage paralleling the bedrooms. It is here that the ghost of Louisa Carteret, one of the ladies in the Bath family, has been repeatedly observed. She has every reason, it appears, to be there. On one occasion she was discovered with a lover by the second Viscount Weymouth, one of Lord Bath's ancestors. A duel was fought by the viscount, and the intruder was killed. Since the viscount had the power of justice

in his domain, there was no need for any inquest. The body of the intruder was hurriedly buried in the cellar. A few years ago, when the present Lord Bath was putting in a boiler, the skeleton of the unfortunate lover was accidentally discovered and removed. But Lady Louisa was forever seen looking for her lost lover, and for all I know she may be looking for him still.

Finally, there is a man of the seventeenth century who has been observed in some of the reception rooms downstairs. According to British medium Trixie Allingham, with whom I worked at Longleat, this is the restless ghost of Sir Thomas Thynne, another of Lord Bath's ancestors. Sir Thomas had the misfortune of being betrayed by his wife, whose lover had hired two professional assassins to murder the husband. This event took place on the highroad, where the murderers stopped a coach bringing Sir Thomas home, dragged him out and killed him. As sometimes happens with ghosts, he was drawn back to where his emotions were, his home, and apparently he cannot find peace because of the tragic events.

With so many ghosts present at Longleat, the chances of running into one or the other are of course considerably higher than if only an occasional specter were to appear at certain times. But don't expect Longleat ghosts to wait upon you just because you paid your entrance fee or had lunch downstairs in the cafeteria. If you can wangle a personal introduction to Lord Bath himself, and a private tour into the nontourist areas, then perhaps you might experience some of the things I have been talking about.

49

Salisbury Hall
St. Albans

About an hour from London, in the direction of St. Albans, Hertfordshire, stands a moderate-sized manor house called Salisbury Hall. The area was settled at a very early period in British history, and within a few miles of where the Roman city of Verulamium stood. Roman artifacts are frequently dug out of the soil in and around Salisbury Hall.

Another noteworthy event was the battle of Barnet during which the hall was a fortified strongpoint. Many soldiers died in and around the house, and swords and bones have been found in the moat and garden.

The ground floor of the manor contains several smaller rooms and a very large and impressive room called the crown chamber, with a fireplace on one side. Next to the fireplace there is a door and beyond it a staircase leading to the upper floor.

The area near this staircase is the spot where a number of witnesses have seen the ghost of Nell Gwyn, favorite of Charles II.

It may strike some of my readers as curious that a ghost can appear in more than one location, but Nell Gwyn apparently was partially free and allowed herself to be drawn back to two places connected with her emotional life. Both her city apartment at 69 Dean Street and this country place held deep and precious memories for her, and it is therefore conceivable that she could have been seen at various times in both places. There was no doubt about the identity of the apparition that has been described by Sir Winston

Churchill's stepfather, Mr. Cornwallis-West. Less illustrious observers have also seen her.

But in addition to the wraith of Nell, there is also the ghost of a cavalier who haunts the upstairs part of the hall. At one time there was an additional wing to the building, which no longer exists. It is in the corridor leading to that nonexistent wing that the cavalier has been observed. In one of the rooms at the end of the corridor, the cavalier is said to have committed suicide when being pursued by soldiers of Oliver Cromwell. He apparently carried some valuable documents and did not want to have them fall into the hands of his pursuers; nor did he want to be tortured into telling them anything of value. This was at the height of the Civil War in England, when the Cavaliers—or partisans of the Royalists—were hotly pursued by the parliamentary soldiers, also known as Roundheads. Although the suicide took place in the 1640s, the footsteps of the ghostly cavalier can still be heard on occasion at Salisbury Hall.

Salisbury Hall belongs to Walter Goldsmith who lives there with his wife and children. He is an artist by profession but has lately turned the hall into a part-time tourist attraction on certain days of the week. Since he has spent great sums of money to restore the manor from the state of disrepair in which he bought it, one can hardly blame him for the modest fee of admission required for a visit. Mr. Goldsmith will gladly point out the haunted spots and discuss psychic phenomena without denying their reality, especially in his house.

50

Sawston Hall
Cambridge

A short distance from the great English university town of Cambridge, off the main road, lies Sawston Hall, a Catholic stronghold that has been in the Huddleston family for many generations. It is an imposing, gray stone structure, three stories high and surrounded by a lovely garden. It is so secluded that it is sometimes hard to locate unless one knows exactly where to turn off the main road. Inside, the great hall is a major accomplishment of Tudor architecture, and there are many large rooms, bedrooms, and galleries. Sawston Hall represents the very best in English Tudor architecture. Its size lies somewhere between the great houses of royalty and the baronial estates which dot the English countryside by the hundreds.

Sawston Hall can be visited by the public on certain days and by prearrangement. The man to contact is Major A.C. Eyre, nephew of the late Captain Huddleston, who manages the estate.

The principal personality associated with Sawston Hall is Queen Mary Tudor, sometimes called Bloody Mary. She rebuilt Sawston Hall after her enemies had burned it down. Her favorite room was a drawing room with a virginal, a sixteenth-century musical instrument.

From the drawing room, one goes through a corridor called the Little Gallery, and a paneled bedroom, into the Tapestry Bedroom which is named for a large set of Flemish tapestries on the wall, depicting the life of King Solomon. In the center of this room is a four-poster in which Queen Mary allegedly slept. In the wall behind the bed is a door through which her ghost is said to have appeared on several occasions. Behind that door lies a passage leading to a so-called priest's hole, a secret hiding place where Roman Catholic priests were hidden during the turbulent times of the religious wars in the sixteenth century. Whenever Protestant raiders came, the priests would hide themselves in these prearranged hiding places which were well supplied with air, water, and food. As soon as everything was clear, the priests would emerge to join the Catholic household.

A number of people who have slept in what is called Queen Mary's room, in the four-poster, have reported uncanny experiences. It is always the same story: three knocks at the door, then the door opens by itself and a gray form slowly floats across the room and disappears into the tapestry. Many have heard the virginal play soft music when there was no one in the drawing room. It is a fact that the young Princess Mary was expert at this instrument, and on numerous occasions was asked to play to show her musical talents.

In 1553, Princess Mary was living in Norfolk, when her half-brother Edward VI died. The Duke of Northumberland, who then dominated the English government, did not want her to succeed to the throne, but wanted instead to have a member of his own family rule England. A false message was sent to Mary purporting to come from her ailing brother Edward. It was in fact a trap set for her by the Duke of Northumberland to lure her to London where he could dispose of her. When Mary reached Sawston Hall on her way to the capital, she received word of the real situation. She immediately fled back to Norfolk. When they discovered that their prey had escaped, the troops of the Duke of Northumberland were enraged and set fire to Sawston Hall. Looking back on the smoldering ruins of Sawston Hall, Mary said to John Huddleston that she would build him a greater hall, once she came to the throne. Not much later she kept her word, and Sawston Hall is the building created during the reign of Mary Tudor. It is not surprising that her spirit should be drawn back to a place that actually saved her life at one time, where she found more love than at any other place in England. Mary Tudor was herself a Catholic, as were the Huddlestons, and thus Sawston Hall does represent the kind of emotional tie I have found to be necessary for ghostly manifestation.

Visitors to the hall may not encounter the ghost of Mary Tudor, but then again, one never knows. There are also other presences in this ancient house, but they seem to be concentrated in the upstairs part. The great hall, the little gallery, and Mary's bedroom are all the domain of "the gray lady."

51

Hermitage Castle
Scotland

The dividing line between Scotland and England is known as border country. It is wild and remote, and the roads are far from good. At night you can very easily get lost there, but it is well worth the drive down from Edinburgh to Hermitage Castle, which is located outside the town of Hawick.

The area has a long history of warfare, even in peacetime. When Scotland and England were not yet joined together as one kingdom, this area was filled with lawlessness, and raids in one or the other direction were common. The lords of the area had a nasty habit of throwing their

enemies into dungeons and letting them die of starvation there. One of the more sinister places in the area, Hermitage was built in the early Middle Ages and has long been associated with the Soulis family. It was here that the Earl of Bothwell, who later became her husband, was visited by Mary Queen of Scots, in 1566.

From the outside the castle looks very much the way it did when it was built in the thirteenth century. It consists of two main towers built of rough stones connected in such a manner that the fortress could withstand almost any attack. The entrance gate was well above ground, to prevent enemies from crashing it. Inside, most of the subdivisions no longer exist; but enough of the castle has been restored so that one can walk about and view what was once a reasonably comfortable dwelling—by early medieval standards.

In those far-off days, nobody trusted his neighbors. Petty wars and family feuds were the rule among the nobles of Scotland. When a neighboring chief sent a group of good-will ambassadors to Hermitage to propose cessation of their long feud, the lord of the manor promptly put the men into a small room without food or water. They died there miserably and their ghosts are said to be among the many who still stalk the ruins.

On another occasion, the ruling Lord Soulis invited a number of local chiefs and nobles to a banquet in honor of the marriage of one of his daughters. Access to the castle was one flight up, not on the ground level. This was a defense measure, so that the castle could be defended by simply pulling up the wooden stairs leading from the ground to the first floor. As soon as the guests had all arrived and were seated in the banquet hall upstairs, the ladder was withdrawn and the gate closed by previous arrangement. The plan was to feed the guests first and murder them afterward.

However, the ladder need not have been withdrawn. As an afterthought Lord Soulis had instructed his cook to put poison into the food of his guests and it worked so well they were all dead before the last course of the banquet.

Individual enemies were not fed first and killed later: they were simply taken below, to the dungeon at the cellar level, which had, and still has, a clammy, cold stone floor made of roughly cut rocks. The most frightening spot in the building is a small hole in the stone floor. Enemies were pushed through this hole into the dungeon below, never to see the light of day again. Even their remains were not removed.

I do not doubt that Hermitage is still covered with impressions from its cruel past. Not only are the unhappy spirits of the victims felt in the atmosphere by anyone sensitive enough to do so, but there is still another reason why Hermitage is considered different from ordinary castles. One of the owners, Lord Soulis, was a black magician and had committed a number of documented atrocities. Finally, the people of the countryside got together and seized him. Taking their inspiration from Lord Soulis' own way of life, they dispatched him in a most frightful manner by tying him with lead bands and then boiling him over a fire. According to the *Blue Guide to Scotland*: "To the E. [of Hermitage] is *Nine Stane Rig*, a hill with a stone circle, where the cruel Lord Soulis is said to have been boiled alive by his infuriated vassals. In reality Lord Soulis died in prison at Dumbarton Castle." But according to local talk his ghost is in evidence still at the castle—especially on the anniversary of his death.

Hermitage Castle can be visited without difficulty or previous arrangement. There is a custodian on the premises who, for a small fee, readily takes you on a guided tour. The house is now a kind of museum. There are no accommodations for sleeping in it, nor would I advise anyone to try.

52

Carlingford Abbey
Ireland

Carlingford Castle and Abbey—or what's left of them, which isn't very much except ruins—stand near the shore of Lough Carlingford in northeastern Ireland, facing England across the sea in one direction, and Northern Ireland in the other. The sea can be quite rough at times in this bay, and there is a certain romantic wildness to the scenery even in the summer. Walking amidst the ruins of what was once an imposing castle and abbey, one gets the feeling of time standing still and also sometimes of an eerie presence. James Reynolds in *More Ghosts in Irish Houses*, reports how an English traveler, who was totally unaware of the haunting reported in these ruins, saw the shadowy figures of a woman and of a man standing in what was once a chapel, only to merge and disappear into the night.

When I visited the ruins of Carlingford with Sybil Leek, she too felt the presence of something unearthly—but to her these ghosts were not frightening or unhappy. Rather she felt a kind of love imprint from the past, something that came and went but somehow was tied to these rocks.

There is a small piece of land between the ruins and the sea, and a road leading down toward it. From the ruined wall of Carlingford all the way down to the shore, seems to be the haunted area, or at any rate the area most likely to give a sensitive person the feeling of a presence.

What is left of Carlingford Castle and Abbey is nothing more than a few stone walls without roofs, and a few impressive arches and glassless windows. What was once the chapel, however, is fairly well preserved even though it has neither roof nor floor, nor in fact anything whatsoever to worship by. The niche about the altar is now empty, but it contained a statute of the Virgin at one time.

Who then are the ghostly figures seen by the English tourist? In the first part of the fifteenth century a lady pirate by the name of Henrietta Travescant, after giving up the sea, retired to Carlingford Abbey to serve as its head. Her ship in her active pirate days had been called *The Black Abbess*, so she took the same name when she became the resident abbess of Carlingford.

Perhaps what had prompted her to give up her cherished sea was not only her patriotic desire to give her

ship to King Henry V, whom she supported, to serve in his war against France, but also her unhappiness at the loss of her beloved Nevin O'Neill, whom the cruel sea had taken during one of their expeditions.

According to the legend as told by James Reynolds, the years passed by and soon the Black Abbess found herself practically alone in the rambling and partially dilapidated castle and abbey at Carlingford. One night when praying in front of the Madonna, she heard the voice of her dead lover calling to her from out of the mist. Not sure of his identity, she is said to have demanded proof that it was really he who was calling out to her. Soon after, she heard him again calling her from the seashore, ran down toward the sea, and was swallowed up by a huge breaker, never to be found again.

It is her ghost, and that of Nevin O'Neill, who have often been seen walking by the rocky seashore or standing together in the ruined chapel. Quiet summer nights, close to midnight, are the best time to run into this phenomenon—if you are one of those who are capable of registering the very tenuous vibrations of such a haunting.

Carlingford is now only a small town, but at one time in the seventeenth century it was large enough to be the temporary capital of Ireland, and a parliament was once in session there. One reaches Carlingford either by railroad to Dundalk and then about eight miles by car over a winding but otherwise good road, or one can go all the way from Dublin by car. Carlingford is equidistant from Dublin and Belfast. The ruins can be reached on foot only, directly from the village. Like so many other Irish towns, its population has dwindled over the years, and it is now actually more like a village than a small town. But the people of Carlingford are still proud of it and prefer to call it a town.

53

Renvyle
Connemara

Today, Renvyle House is a first-rate hotel looking out onto the western-most tip of Ireland. It is the nearest point to the United States. It is cold and windy at times, but during the summer months can be pleasant and warm. The accommodations are first class even though limited, because Renvyle House is not very large as hotels go.

Most of the tourists who come to Renvyle are from England, with an occassional sprinkling of Americans. Originally, the house was owned by the family of Oliver St. John Gogarty, the famous literary figure. The house stood on the site of the original Gogarty House, which burned down during the so-called "Troubles." Although the present structure was built in 1932, it seems to have inherited some of the hauntings of the past.

As soon as the house had been rebuilt, Mr. Gogarty ran it as a kind of hotel for literary figures of his day. W.B. Yeats made it almost a second home. Many séances were held there, and on one such occasion something was dredged up from the past of Renvyle House that wouldn't go away.

Built like a western Irish country manor, the house is white and brown, the bottom part consisting of stone and the top portion of wood. The shingled roof is of a grayish color. To reach it, one must go to Galway and it takes as much as three hours to Renvyle by car since the roads are far from good. But the trip is definitely worthwhile.

Prior to the acquisition of the place by St. John Gogarty, the house had been the seat of the Blake family. The haunted rooms seem to be Number 27, Number 2, and possibly Number 38. It all started after a séance held during the St. John Gogarty ownership of the place, when one of the Blake children evidently materialized before the astonished assembly.

Oliver St. John Gogarty himself reported this incident in an article in *Tomorrow* magazine in 1952. Eoin Dillon, a former manager of Renvyle House, reported that on several occasions people complained that a stranger was in their rooms. What was more, the stranger disappeared rather suddenly, without benefit of a door. Mr. Dillon himself heard finger-clicking noises when he slept in the room once used by Yeats for the séances. He decided to pull the blanket over his ears and let the matter clear itself up. A maid also had seen a man in one of the upstairs corridors disappear before her eyes into thin air. When she described the stranger, it developed that he looked a great deal like the late W.B. Yeats. The apparition was seen about lunchtime in 1966, and one must remember that Yeats did indeed consider Renvyle House a second home. It is entirely conceivable that someone coming to Renvyle House in the future, possessed of the right psychic abilities, might encounter one of those staying behind, beyond flesh and blood—either the Blake boy or perhaps the great poet himself.

54

Kilkea Castle
Kildare

From a distance, Kilkea Castle looks the very image of an Irish castle. Turreted, gray, proud, sticking up from the landscape with narrow and tall windows which give it a massive and fortified appearance, Kilkea Castle is nevertheless one of the most comfortable tourist hotels in present-day Ireland. Anyone may go there simply by making a reservation with the genial host, Dr. William Cade.

The castle is about an hour and a half by car from Dublin, in the middle of fertile farmlands. There are beautiful walks all around it, and the grounds are filled with brooks, old trees, and meadows—the latter populated by a fairly large number of cows.

Kilkea was built in 1180 by an Anglo-Norman knight named Sir Walter de Riddleford, and it is said to be the oldest inhabited castle in Ireland, although I have seen this claim put forward in regard to several places. Let there be no mistake: the inside has been modified and very little of the original castle remains. But the haunting is still there.

The castle has four floors, not counting cellars and roof. The rooms are of varying sizes and kinds. The haunted area is actually what must have been the servants' quarters at one time, and it is reached through a narrow passage in the northern section of the castle. The room itself is just large enough for one person, and if you should want to sleep in it, you had better make a reservation way ahead of time. All you need to do is ask Dr. Cade for the haunted room. He will understand.

The story of the haunting goes back to the early Middle Ages. Apparently one of the beautiful daughters of an early owner fell in love with a stableboy. Her proud father disapproved and threatened to kill them both if they continued their association. One night, the father found the young man in his daughter's room. In the struggle that followed the boy was killed, but we are not told whether the girl was killed or not. But it is the boy's ghost who apparently still roams the corridors, trying to get his sweetheart back.

In the course of rebuilding, this room became part of the servants' quarters. A number of people have reported uncanny feelings in the area. The owner of Kilkea himself, though skeptical, has admitted to witnessing doors opening by themselves for no apparent reason.

Locally, the so-called Wizard Earl is blamed for the happenings at Kilkea Castle, and there is even a legend about him. Apparently to please his lady fair, the earl transformed himself into a bird and sat on her shoulder. But he had not counted on the presence of the castle cat, who jumped up and ate the bird. The legend continues that the earl and his companions still ride at night and will eventually return from the beyond to "put things right in Ireland"—if that is necessary. The legend does not say what happened to the cat.

MOM,

REMEMBER THE DAY July 15, 85,
WHEN WE DANCED TO STAGER LEE & Billie,
AND TAlKED ABOUT REINCARNATION ON
THE PhONE FOR 1½ HOURS!

THESE BOOKS ARE FOR
YOU MY LOVE.

LOVE
SIS